CHINESE ART

in the Royal Ontario Museum

Staff of the Far Eastern Department

Publication of *Chinese Art* was assisted by a grant from The Canada Council

Contents

Introduction — 1

Chronology — 6

Frontispiece — 9

Oracle Bones — 11

Ceramics — 13

Bronze — 79

Tomb Figurines — 117

Sculptures — 147

Painting — 179

Jade — 193

Lacquer — 209

Gold and Silver — 219

Textiles — 231

Introduction

The Royal Ontario Museum's Chinese collections are internationally known. Reproductions and studies of many outstanding objects amongst these have been published in both popular and scholarly literature, frequently and for half a century. Occasionally, we are asked how so extensive and valuable a representation of Chinese archaeological and art historical materials came to Toronto. It seems fitting in this year, the Museum's 60th anniversary Jubilee, to offer a special tribute to those responsible for the wealth of the Far Eastern Department's main holdings.

The present publication does not attempt to offer an archaeological or art historical survey of China. Rather, it is arranged to convey the major strengths of our holdings. Ceramics are pre-eminent and include the greatest number of examples. Bronzes, though less numerous, are among the most ancient and rarest of Chinese artifacts. The Museum's examples are distinguished by virtue of having come almost directly from their sites of discovery, for the most part. Tomb figurines are now prized by Western collectors for their immediacy of representational effect, and by Chinese for their vivid expression of historical mores. At the time the Museum acquired most of its collection in this category, few Westerners even knew what these small sculptures were, while Chinese looked askance at their collection as a result of the desecration of ancestral burials. Other categories are well represented, though with less numerical and, sometimes, aesthetic strength.

Preceding each category in this publication is an essay describing the Museum's most important examples in the medium. Descriptions of individual objects are more technical and intended for the serious student. Since each work is clearly illustrated in reproduction, descriptive details are confined to what might not be visible in the photographs. Publication and other bibliographic references can guide those interested to further study, and to the bases for our identifications of these examples.

Whether fact or myth, it is recorded that the Museum owes its accumulation of Chinese artifacts to a happy chance which befell the first director of the Royal Ontario Museum of Archaeology — Dr. Charles T. Currelly. As an Egyptologist, Dr. Currelly visited Cairo frequently. He acquired two Han Dynasty ceramics in 1908 from an Egyptian dealer who had spent some time in China. His interest was awakened to an area far from his usual specialty. It was maintained by a gift from the Chinese legation in London, in 1911.

It was not until after the First World War that a fortuitous meeting occurred between Dr. Currelly and an English fur merchant *cum* amateur antiquarian, Mr. George Crofts. The latter visited Toronto in 1918 and saw a postcard for sale in his hotel lobby. This he immediately recognized as reproducing an object which he had acquired and sent to a London dealer (see

Charles Trick Currelly

1

No. 111). The ceramic *Lohan* sculpture was identified as being in the ROMA, where Mr. Crofts promptly went and left his card. It was only after some hours that Dr. Currelly realized the importance of meeting a gentleman who had offices in Tientsin and Peking, China, as well as London, England. Thus began an association of eight years, bringing to the Museum its main collections in Chinese ceramics, tomb figurines, painting and sculpture.

Correspondance between Dr. Currelly and Mr. Crofts reveals not only the former's enthusiasm, encouraging further acquisitions even when funds for them were not immediately available, but also the latter's generosity and self-sacrifice, often paying for desirable items out of his own pocket and accepting reimbursement of cost alone, and travelling to the interior of China on horseback on arduous searches sometimes covering 140 *li* (*c.* 47 English miles) in a day. Mr. Crofts warned, after his first shipment of 978 pieces in November, 1918 —

War conditions are now at an end in China and prices have very greatly advanced. Apart from this the goods are scarce and not coming in or available in the interior. You have sufficient now for a dozen museums.

Nevertheless, shipments continued, with their record as follows —

June 1919 — 66 cases / Dec. 1920 — 30 cases / Aug. 1921 — 49 cases / Dec. 1921 — 21 cases.

Mr. Crofts' contacts were mainly with Chinese merchants in Honan and Shansi provinces. As a result, the Museum's ceramics, both vessels and tomb figurines, show their best representation in products of those two regions. The two men did not always agree in what each considered important for the Museum. Mr. Crofts was first interested in ceramics and paintings "in Chinese taste," but Dr. Currelly informed him in July, 1922 — "...sculpture is *the* big thing." This attitude was perhaps natural to an Egyptologist, but Mr. Crofts replied in March, 1923 —

I feel that Sung porcelains are going to be the treasures for a collector, whilst the Stone Tablets (?, perhaps referring to Buddhist sculpture) will always be merely museum pieces and for the archaeologist or scientist, whereas the othe pieces will be educational and for the people.

After 1922, treasure hunting became more difficult in China. On July 10th, 1922, the Chinese government's Board of Interior issued a proclamation prohibiting the export of Chinese antiquities. By the following year, both Chinese and Japanese dealers were ignoring the law, and contacting London and Paris directly with offers of Sung porcelains, bronzes, and sculpture in stone and wood. Mr. Crofts continued to help the Museum and, from 1923, extended his advice to Mr. Langdon Warner, the famous Harvard University professor of Chinese art history, who was then helping the Philadelphia

George Crofts

Museum of Art to form its collections. Toronto was not unaware of the great benefaction given to it by Mr. Crofts. An LL.D. *honoris causa* was conferred upon him by the University of Toronto in June, 1922. Dr. Currelly reported on the Museum of Archaeology for 1923-1924—

The George Crofts Collection is so far in advance of any other known collection of early Chinese art that we will probably hold our supremacy in this great field.

Scarcely had Mr. Crofts become less active in the Museum's service, due to business adversities and ill health, when another unique opportunity in the Chinese field presented itself to Dr. Currelly. The Reverend William C. White was designated Anglican Bishop of Honan province. As a Torontonian, Bishop White was considered by Dr. Currelly to be a natural for the task of continuing acquisitions from China for the Museum. He wrote to the Bishop in October, 1926 —

I am convinced that the grip of Chinese art will become stronger and stronger on Europe and America, and that this is the next great coming study in the artistic-historical field.

Not unnaturally, the Bishop's first duty was to his church work, at that time involving the immense task of famine relief for the impoverished area of his diocese. He was, however, a trained scholar, and met the Museum's challenge with characteristic energy and method, meeting and learning from experienced American sinologists in Peking. By March, 1929, he had formulated his own interests to the extent that he could write to Dr. Currelly —

You desire to lay more emphasis on the aesthetic and attractive aspects of specimens for the Museum. I shall bear this in mind in the future, for I am afraid I have been thinking more of the cultural and technical aspects.

In January, 1925, Bishop White had sent a shipment of Sung Dynasty ceramics, and bronze fragments including chariot parts and weapons which he later recognized to be of the Shang and Chou dynasties. His first shipment of Chinese Judaica was sent in September, 1925, and led eventually to his publication *Chinese Jews*, 3 vols. (Toronto: Univ. Press, 1942, 2nd ed. 1966), which remains the definitive work on this subject. Forty boxes of bronzes arrived from the Bishop in 1927, the famous Yüan Dynasty wall-paintings (see No. 118) in 1929, Han Dynasty tomb tiles (see No. 117) in the same year, and other shipments through the following year. By this time Dr. Currelly had realized that the Bishop's competence in Chinese went far beyond that of the interested dilettante. He began, in 1931, to encourage the establishment of a professorship in Chinese at the University of Toronto, apparently with the Bishop in mind. Meanwhile, the Museum's financial situation had worsened. When Dr. Currelly wrote in August 1932 that further buying was impossible, the Bishop answered that he would accept the financial responsibility himself. Bishop White returned to

Bishop William C. and Mrs. White

Toronto after further endeavours in China were made impossible in the turbulent conditions of north China. By April 24th, 1934, he had become the first Professor of Chinese at the University of Toronto, and defined his sphere of interest as archaeology, defining it in an interview reported in the Toronto Daily Star as— ... *the study of the life and culture of a people through early art effects.*

At the same time, he became the first Keeper of East Asiatic Art in the Museum of Archaeology, and began his dozen years of immensely fruitful scholarship in Chinese studies. His many publications remain as ever living and useful monuments to his abilities and service.

It was through the Bishop that the third main benefactor to the Museum's Chinese collections became active. The Reverend Dr. James M. Menzies served as a missionary of the Presbyterian Church of Canada near An-yang, Honan province. This area, later recognized to be the site of the last Shang Dynasty capital, has always been rich in antiquities. Dr. Menzies began collecting for the Museum in 1931, though he had realized the importance of his location as early as 1914. He had formulated an important collection of China's earliest historical documents, Shang Dynasty divination or oracle bones with inscriptions in archaic script, for himself, but this was lost in 1927 during the looting of the so-called "second revolution." However, Dr. Menzies returned to gather a second collection, now in large part at the Museum (see Frontispiece). Between 1938 and 1941 Dr. Menzies was a Research Assistant in this Department of the Museum, under the auspices of the Rockefeller Foundation; his work culminating in publication of the monograph *The Shang Ko* (Toronto: ROM, 1965). The Museum is also the fortunate recipient of the Menzies collection comprising many artifacts—bronzes, ceramic sherds, etc. The Menzies Trust Fund now supports scholarship in Chinese archaeology, and is responsible for the catalogue—*The Menzies Collection of Oracle Bones*, Vol. I (Toronto: ROM, 1972), Vol. II to follow.

Two successors to Bishop White as keepers of the Far Eastern Department, as we are now titled and the rank as Curator, have contributed their special knowledge to study and understanding of our collections. Miss Helen E. Fernald joined the Museum as Assistant to the Keeper in 1944. Her particular contributions were in the fields of sculpture and textiles, producing many articles and other studies on examples in our, as well as other, collections. Mr. Henry Trubner became Curator in 1958. His reputation as a specialist in ceramics found a receptive Toronto and Museum. The immense success of his many exhibitions in aspects of Chinese, as well as Japanese and Korean art, brought fresh interest in Asia to Canadians as a whole.

The present incumbent assumed the post in 1968. She hopes to be able to strengthen our Chinese holdings in those areas of its weakness, notably in

Dr. James M. Menzies at his graduation. Photo courtesy The United Church Archives, Victoria College

painting and sculpture, and to expand the Department's coverage to sounder ground for Japan, Korea, South-East Asia and the Indian sub-continent.

Hsio-Yen Shih, Curator
June 1972

Chronology	Period Name	Dates	Major Art Forms
	Late Neolithic	?3000-1500 B.C.	*Ceramics*—painted and black earthenware.
	Shang (or Yin)	*?1500-1028* B.C.	*Ceramics*—grey and white earthenware. *Bronzes*—ceremonial vessels, weapons. *Carved bone, jade* and *stone.*
	Chou Western Chou	?1027-771 B.C.	*Ceramics*—grey and glazed earthenware. *Bronzes*—ceremonial vessels, implements and weapons. *Carved jade.*
	Eastern Chou	770-222 B.C.	*Ceramics*—grey earthenware. *Bronzes*—bells and mirrors; small objects, including chariot fittings, inlaid with precious and semi-precious materials. *Carved jade.* *Lacquer wares.* * The beginnings of pictorial decoration.
	Ch'in	221-207 B.C.	as in preceding period
	Han Western Han	206 B.C.- A.D. 8	*Ceramics*—painted grey earthenware; tomb tiles; tomb figurines. *Bronzes*—mirrors; small sculptures; small objects. *Carved jade.* *Lacquer wares.*
	Eastern Han including Interregnum	A.D. 9-220	*Ceramics*—lead-glazed earthenware and feldspathic-glazed stoneware tomb figurines. *Bronzes*—as in preceding period.

Carved jade.
Lacquer wares.
Monumental sculpture.
Painted scrolls (no longer extant).

Six Dynasties Period 220-589   *Ceramics*—Yüeh ware; tomb figurines.
Buddhist painting and sculpture.

Sui   589-618   *Ceramics*—white- and green-glazed porcellaneous stoneware; tomb figurines.
Buddhist sculpture.

T'ang   618-906   *Ceramics*—three-colour glazed earthenware; white-glazed porcelain; tomb figurines.
Bronzes—mirrors.
Carved jade.
Lacquer wares.
Gold and *silver*—vessels and ornaments.
Buddhist painting and *sculpture.*
Secular painted scrolls and *screens.*
Architecture and *city-planning.*

Five Dynasties   906-1279   *Ceramics*—"Tz'u-chou" type folk wares.
Landscape painting.

Sung
Northern Sung   960-1126   *Ceramics*—green-glazed porcellaneous stoneware (celadon); carved and moulded decoration on many types.
Lacquer wares.
Gold and *silver*—vessels and ornaments.
Painting—beginning of imperial painting academy.

Ceramics

China's pre-eminent position in ceramic technology has long been recognized throughout the world. The beauty and fine quality of the products of Chinese kilns have been appreciated in Japan since the T'ang Dynasty, and in the Sung vast quantities of celadon and *ch'ing-pai* vessels were exported all over south-east Asia. Arab traders first brought celadons and the highly prized underglazed blue and white to the Middle East, while Portuguese and Dutch carried Chinese porcelain to Europe where the secret of its production tantalized European potters. The Chinese ceramics in the ROM were acquired primarily through the efforts of Mr. George Crofts and Bishop William C. White. Our collection of glazed wares dating from the Shang (see No. 3) to the Ch'ing Dynasty, taken in conjunction with the unglazed vessels and sherds from the Neolithic period (see No. 2) to the Han Dynasty, offers a comprehensive picture of the development of this craft.

The number and variety of some groups make them of special interest to students. Of particular importance is the Museum's collection of wares of the Tz'u-chou family. The name is derived from the county name of Tz'u Hsien, Hopei Province, but similar white-slipped, buff or grey-bodied stonewares for general use were produced in kilns throughout north China. The large collection includes vessels and pillows (see No. 27) dating from the Sung to Ming Dynasty, and is comprehensive, containing three-colour and dark-glazed pieces (see No. 32) and many undecorated white vessels. Its strength lies in its range of decorated vessels, some of unusual shape (see No. 25). These painted, incised or carved pieces date from the 10th to 16th centuries and display much regional variation in decoration.

The green and white wares of the finer branch of the feldspathic-glazed tradition are also well represented. The history of celadon can be traced from Han proto-porcelain (see No. 14) through its development in south China in the Six Dynasties, T'ang (see No. 17) and Five Dynasties periods to its flowering in Chechiang province in the Sung Dynasty (see No. 18). The collection also contains a number of the larger, heavier pieces from the period of its gradual decline in the Yüan and Ming dynasties. Although celadon was primarily a southern development, its influence was felt in the north. Some early examples from northern centres in the Sui Dynasty (see No. 16) and fine products of the Sung Dynasty Yao-chou kilns of Shensi province (see No. 19) are included in the collection.

While southern kilns concentrated on the development of celadon, northern kilns devoted their creative energies to white ware and there is an excellent study collection of such Sui and T'ang stonewares, displaying considerable variation in shape, glaze and body (see Nos. 21 & 22). The crowning achievement of the ceramic industry at this time, however, was the successful firing of true porcelain, and the Museum possesses an elegant porcelain stem-cup of T'ang Dynasty date (see No. 38).

White-bodied wares continued to be refined and at Ching-te-chen in Kiangsi province a new ware came into being in the 11th century. The Museum has a good collection of this pale blue-glazed ware called *ch'ing-pai* which rapidly became popular for vessels (see Nos. 39 & 40) and Buddhist sculpture (see No. 41). Because of the demands of the export trade, the manufacture of *ch'ing-pai* spread to coastal kilns, while at Ching-te-chen developments in body and glaze and the introduction of the technique of underglaze painting in cobalt culminated in the production of blue and white in the Yüan Dynasty. Although the Museum has a few fine examples from the 15th century (see Nos. 43 & 44), its strength lies in the 16th and 17th centuries (see Nos. 45, 47-49).

The lead-glazed wares of the collection also provide ample opportunity for study. The Han and T'ang periods are particularly well represented. There are many Han green-glazed vessels (see No. 8) and tomb models and a fine selection of T'ang three-colour glazed pieces (see No. 10). The continuation of this tradition can be traced through pieces from the Liao (see No. 30) and Sung dynasties (see No. 26). There are good examples from the Ming Dynasty (see No. 12), including a large number of roof tiles.

With its excellent range of vessels from all periods and traditions of Chinese ceramic history, and the wealth of its research material in certain specific areas, the Chinese ceramic collecton is a source of pride to the Museum.

Mino Yutaka & Patricia Proctor

Detail from entry number 23

1. Mortuary Jar
Coil-made earthenware; soft buff-pink
body decorated in black (manganese)
and red (haematite) pigments.
Ht. 14⅞" (37.7 cm.)
930.20.4

Neolithic, Kansu "Yang-shao" phase,
"Pan-shan" stage.
Provenance:
Dr. A. Goffin, Brussels, Belgium;
Mrs. George (E.M.) Sarton, Cambridge,
Mass.
Reportedly uncovered near the
western border of Kansu province by a
European. Similar vessels from the
same find are in the Fogg Art Museum,
Harvard University, Cambridge, Mass.;
and the Cleveland Museum of Art,
Ohio.

Published:
H. Trubner, *The Far Eastern Collection*
(Toronto: ROM, 1968), p. 24 no. 14.
Cf. N. Palmgren, *Kansu Mortuary Urns
of the Pan Shan and Ma Chang Groups*,
"Palaeonotologia Sinica, Series D, III: 1"
(Peking, 1934), Pl. XVI fig. 2.

2. Mortuary Jar
Coil-made earthenware; soft buff body
decorated in black (manganese) and
red (haematite) pigments.
Ht. 9⅛" (23.2 cm.)
930.20.1

Neolithic, Kansu "Yang-shao" phase,
"Pan-shan" stage.
Found and acquired with 930.20.4
(No. 1)

Published:
"West-East," ROMA *Bulletin*, No. 21 (Oct.
1953), no. 40;
T.A. Heinrich, *Art Treasures in the*
(Toronto, 1963), p. 30;
H. Trubner, *The Far Eastern Collection*
(Toronto: ROM, 1968), p. 24 no. 15.

16

3. Jar

Grey ware, coil-made hard-fired earthenware; body burnt brown and covered from shoulder to foot with thin uneven layer of clear glaze from ash fluxing agent.
Ht. 8-5/16" (21.1 cm.)
960.238.35

Shang Dynasty, An-yang period (c. 1300-1028 B.C.)
Provenance:
Dr. James M. Menzies Collection
From An-yang, Honan province.

Published:
B. Stephen, "Some Chinese Archaeological Discoveries in the Menzies Collection," ROM *Annual* (1962), pp. 59-60, Pl. XXV;
T.A. Heinrich, *Art Treasures in the ROM* (Toronto, 1963), p. 30;
H. Trubner, *The Far Eastern Collection* (Toronto: ROM, 1968), p. 17 no. 8.
Cf. Li Chi, "Studies of the Hsiao-T'un Pottery: Yin and Pre-Yin," *Annals of Academia Sinica*, No. 2 Part I (Taipei, May 1955), pp. 103-117

4. Pedestalled Bowl *(kuei)*

Grey ware, wheel-made earthenware; decoration incised or impressed.
Ht. 8½" (21.5 cm.)
960.238.39

Late Shang or early Chou Dynasty, c. 1100-900 B.C.
Provenance:
Dr. James M. Menzies Collection

Published:
H. Trubner, *The Far Eastern Collection* (Toronto: ROM, 1968), p. 5 no. 3.
Cf. *Sekai Kōkogaku Taikei,* Vol. 6 (Tokyo: Heibonsha, 1959), p. 112. fig. 325, for a similar example excavated from Tomb 150 at Liu-li-ko, Hui Hsien, Honan province, in a later Shang Dynasty context;
K'ao-ku hsüeh-pao, No. 8 (1954), p. 114 fig. 6, Pl. 5, for similar examples from P'u-tu-ts'un, Sian, Shensi province, in Western Chou Dynasty contexts.

5. **Wine Bowls** *(erh-pei)*

Grey ware, mould-made earthenware; thin sandy body, exterior iridescent with mica coating, interior washed with cinnabar pigment.
Ht. 1¼" (3.2 cm.), l. 4" (10.2 cm.), w. 3⅝" (9.2 cm.)
923.1.1 a & b

Former Han Dynasty, *c.* 1st century B.C.
Provenance:
George Crofts Collection

6. **Lampstand**

Grey ware, wheel-made earthenware; applied decoration of hand-modelled free figures; remains of white (calcite), red (cinnabar) and black (carbon) pigments on exterior.
Ht. 14¼" (36 cm.), diam. at base 19⅛" (45.8 cm.)
944.24

Later Han Dynasty, A.D., 2nd century.
Cf. *K'ao-ku t'ung-hsun*, 1957 no. 4, Pl. 5:1, for an example excavated from Tomb 8 at Shen Hsien, Honan province, which is more complete. Its oil lamp proper is an independent vessel, bowl-like in shape with a phoenix-head on one edge balanced by a bird-tail handle.

9. Lion Statuette

Earthenware; pinkish body with creamy-white lead glaze, now partially iridescent with decomposition; form hand-modelled and carved, with head perhaps mould-made.
Ht. 9½" (24.1 cm.)
918.21.397

T'ang Dynasty, 7th-8th century.
Provenance:
George Crofts Collection.
Reportedly from Chang-te Fu (i.e. near An-yang), Honan province.

Published:
T. Kobayashi, *Tōsō no hakuji,* ("Tōki Zenshū Vol. 12" (Tokyo: Heibonsha, 1959), Pl. 4;
H. Trubner, *The Far Eastern Collection* (Toronto: ROM, 1968), p. 51 no. 60.
Compare to lion statuette in marble (933.12.4), see No. 106.

10. Ewer

Three-colour glazed earthenware; buff body covered with mottled and streaked green, yellow and transparent glazes; applied decoration of moulded reliefs.
Ht. 9½" (24.15 cm.)
920.1.83

T'ang Dynasty, 7th-8th century.
Provenance:
George Crofts Collection.
Reportedly from Lo-yang, Honan province.

Published:
O. Sirén, *Kinas Konst under tre Artusenden* (Stockholm: Esselte Aktiebolag, 1943), Vol. II, fig. 229;
"West-East," ROMA *Bulletin,* no. 21 (Oct. 1953), no. 115;
T. Dexel, *Die Formen chinesischer Keramik* (Tübingen: Wasmuth, 1955), Pl. 49b;
The Arts of the T'ang Dynasty (Los Angeles County Museum, 1957), no. 186;
M. Prodan, *The Art of the T'ang Potter* (London: Thames and Hudson, 1960), Pl. 109;
M. Sullivan, *Introduction to Chinese Art* (London: Faber, 1961), Pl. 81;
H. Trubner, *The Far Eastern Collection* (Toronto: ROM, 1968), p. 46 no. 50.

11. Rhyton

Three-colour glazed earthenware;
white body with amber glaze on
exterior, and mottled amber, green
and cream glazes on interior;
moulded decoration.
Ht. 2 15/16" (7.45 cm.), l. 4½"
(11.45 cm.)
920.20.1

T'ang Dynasty, 7th-8th century.
Provenance:
George Crofts Collection.

Published:
"West-East," ROMA *Bulletin,* No. 21 (Oct.
1953), no. 120;
The Arts of the T'ang Dynasty (Los
Angeles County Museum, 1957),
no. 215;
H. Trubner, *The Far Eastern Collection*
(Toronto: ROM, 1968), p. 49 no. 55.

12. **Tripod Censer** *(ting)*

Three-colour glazed earthenware;
buff body decorated with carved and
applied high relief figures, dragons,
lotus blossoms and monster heads;
glazed in green, yellow and cream.
Inscription in brown glaze on inside
face of handle with date to the 15th
day of the 8th lunar moon in 1469.
Ht. 27½" (70 cm.)
950.88.8

Ming Dynasty, Ch'eng-hua period,
dated to 1469.
Cf. *Wen Wu*, 1956 no. 7, pp. 28-35,
for discussion of Shansi province's
glazed earthenware, with a tripod
censer dated to 1308 on p. 29; also
1962 nos. 4-5, pp. 73-79.

13. **Jar** *(kuan)*
San-ts'ai (fa-hua) ware,
porcellaneous stoneware; inner
container covered by outer
reticulated case; decoration carved
and incised on surface, then glazed in
turquoise, aubergine and cream.
Ht. 13⅜" (33.9 cm.)
939.35

Ming Dynasty, first half of the 16th
century.

Published:
H. Trubner, *The Far Eastern Collection*
(Toronto: ROM, 1968), p. 69 no. 87.

14. Jar *(hu)*

Stoneware; lower body burnt reddish-brown, upper body decorated with incised and stippled patterns under olive-green feldspathic glaze.
Ht. 15-3/16" (38.5 cm.)
920.1.182

Later Han Dynasty (A.D. 25-220).
Provenance:
George Crofts Collection.

Published:
H. Trubner, *The Far Eastern Collection* (Toronto: ROM, 1968), p. 37 no. 38.

Cf. W. Hochstadter, "Pottery and Stoneware of Shang, Chou, and Han," *Bulletin of the Museum of Far Eastern Antiquities,* Stockholm, No. 24 (1952), pp. 98-103, fig. 115, where similar vessels are identified as from Sian, Shensi province;
D. Lion-Goldschmidt and J. Moreau-Gobard, *Chinese Art,* Vol. I (New York: Universe, 1960), tr. by Diana Imber, Pl. 169, where this ware is described as "proto-porcelain" because of its kaolin content;
Wen-wu ts'an-k'ao tzu-liao, 1958 no. 7, p. 63 fig. 4, for a vessel of almost identical form excavated from a Later Han Dynasty tomb at San-li-ts'un, Sian.

15. Jar *(hu)*
Stoneware; heavy reddish body
covered on upper part with olive-
brown feldspathic glaze.
Ht. 15-13/32" (39.1 cm.)
926.21.168

Later Han Dynasty (A.D. 25-220).
Provenance:
Bishop W.C. White Collection.

Published:
H. Trubner, *The Far Eastern Collection*
(Toronto: ROM, 1968), p. 38 no. 39.

Shou-chou, Huai-nan-shih, Anhui
province.

16. Vase
Early Northern Celadon type
stoneware; hard white body with light
olive-green transparent glaze
coarsely crackled.
Ht. 12⅛" (31.5 cm.)
921.1.131.

Sui Dynasty, late 6th-early 7th
century.
Provenance:
George Crofts Collection.
Cf. *K'ao-ku t'ung-hsun,* 1957 no. 3, Pl.
9:2, for a similar example excavated
from the Feng family tombs at Ching
Hsien, Hopei province, where five
epitaph stones dated to the 6th
century were found;
K'ao Ku, 1959 no. 9, pp. 471-472, Pl.
3:14, for a comparable example
excavated from the tomb of Li Ching-
hsün (died 608) in the western
suburbs of Sian, Shensi province;
Wen Wu, 1961 no. 12, pp. 60-66, for
an early Northern Celadon kiln site at

17. Ewer
Wa-cha-p'ing ware, stoneware; buff
body covered with pale green glaze
stopping short of foot; decorated with
applied floral, fish and figural reliefs
covered by circles of brown glaze.
Ht. 7-3/16" (18.3 cm.)
921.21.120

T'ang Dynasty, 8th-9th century.
Provenance:
George Crofts Collection.
Cf. *Wen Wu,* 1960 no. 3, p. 31 fig. 5,
pp. 67-74 and 84, for reports on
investigations of the kilns at Wa-cha-
p'ing and T'ung-kuan in Ch'ang-sha,
Hunan province.

18. Vase (*mei-p'ing* form)
Early Chechiang Celadon,
porcellaneous stoneware; light grey
body with carved and combed
decoration under yellow-green glaze.
Ht. 7¾" (19.7 cm.)
922.20.101

Sung Dynasty, 11th century.
Provenance:
George Crofts Collection.

Published:
J. Wirgin, "Sung Ceramic Designs,"
*Bulletin of the Museum of Far Eastern
Antiquities,* Stockholm, No. 42
(1970), p. 79, Pl. 37h.

20. Dish
Northern Celadon of Yao-chou type, porcellaneous stoneware; greyish-green glaze over carved decoration.
Ht. 1-11/16"(4.3 cm.), diam. 8-1/16" (20.5 cm.)
921.21.133

Sung Dynasty, 11th-12th century.
Provenance:
George Crofts Collection. Reportedly from Lao-yang Hsien (*sic,* Lo-yang?), Honan province.

Published:
J. Wirgin, "Sung Ceramic Designs," *Bulletin of the Museum of Far Eastern Antiquities,* Stockholm, No. 42 (1970), p. 30, Pl. 4e.

21. Amphora
White ware, porcellaneous stoneware; greyish-white body covered with very fine whitish slip and finely crackled pale greenish-white transparent glaze on upper two-thirds of body.
Ht. 21⅛" (53.5 cm.)
914.7.106

Sui or early T'ang Dynasty, late 6th-7th century.

22. Candlestick
White ware, porcellaneous stoneware; white body covered with fine white slip and finely crackled yellowish-white glaze stopping just above base.
Ht. 11⅞" (29.9 cm.), diam. of base

6⅝" (16.85 cm.)
930.65.3

T'ang Dynasty, 8th century.

Published:
T.A. Heinrich, *Art Treasures in the* ROM (Toronto, 1963), p. 58;
H. Trubner, *The Far Eastern Collection* (Toronto: ROM, 1968), p. 50 no. 58.

23. Vase

Tz'u-chou type ware, porcellaneous stoneware; grey body with greyish-white glaze.
Ht. 13" (33.1 cm.)
923.18.14

Five Dynasties period, 10th century.
Provenance:
George Crofts Collection. Reportedly from Shun-te Fu, now Hsing-t'ai Hsien, Hopei province.

Published:
T. Dexel, *Die Formen chinesisches Keramik* (Tübingen: Wasmuth, 1955), Pl. 38a;
The Arts of the T'ang Dynasty (Los Angeles County Museum, 1957), Pl. 218;
M. Prodan, *The Art of the T'ang Potter* (London: Thames and Hudson, 1960), Pl. 117;
T.A. Heinrich, *Art Treasures in the ROM* (Toronto, 1963), p. 58;
H. Trubner, *The Far Eastern Collection* (Toronto: ROM, 1968), p. 50 no. 57.

Cf. *Chōsen Koseki Zufu*, Vol. VIII (Tokyo: Kokka, 1925), Pl. 1132 nos. 3728 & 3729, for examples in Korean collections;
Sekai Tōji Zenshū, Vol. 10 (Tokyo: Zauho, 1955), Col. Pl. 11, for a similar vessel in the Hakone Art Museum, Japan, which is identified as from the Tang-yang-yü kilns at Hsiu-wu Hsien, Honan province;
Hasebe Gakuji, *So no Jishuyō*, "Toki Zenshū Vol. 13" (Tokyo: Heibonsha, 1958), Col. Pl. 4, Pls. 38 and 39.

24. Bowl

Tz'u-chou type ware, porcellaneous stoneware; marbled decoration in brown and white clays with transparent over-all glaze.
Ht. 1½" (3.8 cm.), diam. at mouth 3-7/16" (8.7 cm.)
923.18.1

Sung Dynasty, 11th-12th century.
Provenance:
George Crofts Collection.

25. Hand-Drum
Tz'u-chou ware of Kuan-t'ai type,
stoneware; grey body, exterior first
covered with white slip, then with
black slip cut away and incised to form
decoration of peonies and foliate
scrolls, and finally with transparent
glaze.
L. 14-11/16" (37.24 cm.), diam. of
head 6-11/16" (16.9 cm.)
920.1.209

Sung Dynasty (960-1279).
Provenance:
George Crofts Collection.

Published:
H. Trubner, *The Far Eastern Collection*
(Toronto: ROM, 1968), p. 56 no. 67;
Cf. *Ku-kung po-wu-yuan ts'ang tz'u
hsüan-chi* (Peking, 1962), Pl. 9, for a
hand-drum in Huang-tao ware of the
T'ang Dynasty;
Sekai Tōji Zenshū, Vol. 10 (Tokyo:
Zauho, 1955), Pl. 116, for another
Tz'u-chou type example of the Sung
Dynasty;
Wen Wu, 1959 no. 6, pp. 59-61;
1964 no. 8, pp. 37-48; for report of
excavations at Kuan-t'ai kilns, Honan
province.

26. Pillow

Tz'u-chou ware of Tang-yang-yü type,
eathenware; pink-buff body with
white slip; decoration incised and
glazed with green, yellow and
transparent glazes.
Ht. 5⅜" (13.7 cm.), l. 15¾" (40 cm.).
918.21.501

Sung Dynasty (960-1279)
Provenance:
George Crofts Collection.

Published:
H. Trubner, *The Far Eastern Collection*
(Toronto: ROM, 1968), p. 64 no. 78.
Cf. *Wen-wu ts'an-k'ao tzu-liao,* 1954
no. 4, pp. 44-47, for discussion of
Tang-yang-yü kilns in Hsiu-wu Hsien,
Honan province.

27. Pillow

Tz'u-chou type Honan ware, stoneware; reddish body covered with creamy-white slip; decorated with motifs incised through slip against ground of circles stamped in slip, these filled in with light brown slip, and the whole covered with transparent glaze.
Ht. 4-15/16" (12.6 cm.), l. 10½" (26.7 cm.).
918.21.392

Sung Dynasty, 12th century.
Provenance:
George Crofts Collection. Reportedly from Lo-yang, Honan province.

Published:
H.E. Fernald, "Chinese Mortuary Pillows in the Royal Ontario Museum of Archaeology," *Far Eastern Ceramic Bulletin*, IV:1 (March 1952), p. 11, Pl. VI fig. 14;
J. Wirgin, "Sung Ceramic Designs," *Bulletin of the Museum of Far Eastern Antiquities*, Stockholm, No. 42 (1970), p. 93, Pl. 42e.
Cf. *Wen Wu*, 1964 no. 2, pp. 54-62, Pl. 5:4; 1964 no. 3, pp. 45, 47-55; for report of kiln site investigations at Mi and Teng-feng Hsien, Honan province, with similar wares.

28. **Vase** *(mei-p'ing)*
Tz'u-chou type ware in style of Shansi
province, porcellaneous stoneware;
buff body with white slip, decoration
first incised in outline through slip
then glazed in brown with details
incised through both glaze and slip.
Ht. 13-7/16" (34.1 cm.)
918.21.395

Sung Dynasty, 12th-13th century.
Provenance:
George Crofts Collection.

Published:
H. Trubner, *The Far Eastern Collection*
(Toronto: ROM, 1968), p. 55 no. 66.
Cf. Ch'en Wan-li, *Sung-tai pei-fang
min-chien tz'u-ch'i* (Peking: Ch'ao-
hua mei-shu, 1955), Pl. 22, for an
almost identical vessel from Shansi;
Wen-wu ts'an-k'ao tzu-liao, 1955 no.
9, pp. 148-149, for three similar
ceramics found in a site at Hsia-chia-
kou, T'ien-chen Hsien, Shansi, called
Liao-Chin (916-1234) in this brief
report.

29. Ewer

Earthenware; buff-pink body covered with first white slip then green glaze; incised and impressed decorative patterns, applied plaque with moulded relief.
Ht. 4-25/32" (12.1 cm.)
959.84

Liao Dynasty (916-1124).

Published:
H. Trubner, *The Far Eastern Collection* (Toronto: ROM, 1968), p. 63 no. 77; Y. Mino, "Some Aspects of the Development of Liao Dynasty Ceramics," *Oriental Art,* XVII :3 (Autumn 1971), p. 249, Pl.6.

30. Phoenix-headed Vase

Earthenware; brick-red body covered with first white slip then transparent glaze; both slip and glaze cut away and incised for peony sprays on shoulder; the decorative zone finally covered with transparent green glaze.
Ht. 16-7/8" (42.8 cm.)
918.21.472

Liao Dynasty (916-1124).
Provenance:
George Crofts Collection. Reportedly from Chang-te Fu (i.e. near An-yang), Honan province.

Published:
H. Trubner, *The Far Eastern Collection* (Toronto: ROM, 1968), p. 65 no. 79; Y. Mino, "Some Aspects of the Development of Liao Dynasty Ceramics," *Oriental Art,* XVII:3 (Autumn 1971), p. 247, Pl. 3.

31. **Jar**
Huang-tao ware, stoneware; hard
light grey body covered with
brownish-black glaze ending
unevenly above foot and decorated
with splashes of purplish to bluish-
grey glaze on upper body.
Ht. 8-13/16" (22.3 cm.)
930.65.1

T'ang Dynasty, 8th century.
Cf. C.C. Riely, *Chinese Art from the
Cloud Wampler and other Collections
in the Everson Museum* (Syracuse:
Museum of Art, 1968), no. 25, for a
discussion of this ware from the
Huang-tao kilns at Chia Hsien, Honan
province.

32. **Vase** (depressed *mei-p'ing* form)
Tz'u-chou ware, stoneware; buff body
with "tea-dust" or dark olive glaze,
decorated on shoulder with leaf-
scrolls painted with vitreous slip of
deep blue tone.
Ht. 8-7/32" (20.9 cm.)
918.21.396

Sung Dynasty (960-1279)
Provenance:
George Crofts Collection. Reportedly
from Lao-yang Hsien (*sic,* i.e.
Lo-yang?), Honan province.

Published:
H. Trubner, *The Far Eastern Collection*
(Toronto: ROM, 1968), p. 58 no. 69.

33. Bowl
Tz'u-chou type ware, porcellaneous
stoneware; greyish-white body with
black glaze and "oil-spot" markings.
Ht. 3-11/16" (9.3 cm.), diam. at
mouth 6⅛" (15.6 cm.)
931.13.190

Sung Dynasty, 12th-13th century.
Provenance:
Bishop W.C. White Collection.
Gift of Mrs. H.D. Warren.

34. Covered Bowl
Ting ware, porcelain with reddish-
brown glaze.
Ht. 2⅞" (7.3 cm.), diam. at mouth 3-
7/16" (8.35 cm.)
921.21.130

Sung Dynasty (960-1270)
Provenance:
George Crofts Collection.

Published:
T.A. Heinrich, *Art Treasures in the ROM*
(Toronto, 1963), p. 59;
H. Trubner, *The Far Eastern Collection*
(Toronto: ROM, 1968), p. 59 no. 71.

35. Tea-bowl
Chien ware, porcellaneous
stoneware; grey-black body with
black glaze and "hare's fur" markings.
Ht. 2½" (6.4 cm.), diam. at mouth 5"
(12.7 cm.)
963.141.13

Sung Dynasty (960-1279)
Provenance:

J.M. Plumer Collection.

Published:
H. Trubner, *The Far Eastern Collection*
(Toronto: ROM, 1968), p. 60 no. 73.

36. **Vase** *(mei-p'ing)*
Stoneware with dark brown glaze;
decorated with horizontal wheel
ribbing.
Ht. 17¾" (45.05 cm.)
926.21.93

Liao Dynasty (960-1124)
Provenance:
Bishop W.C. White Collection.

Published:
H. Trubner, *The Far Eastern Collection*
(Toronto: ROM, 1968), p. 65 no. 80.

37. **Jar** (lotus bud form)
Chün ware, porcellaneous stoneware;
lavender-grey glaze with bright purple
splashes.
Ht. 3-5/16" (8.35 cm.)
931.18.11

Sung Dynasty (960-1279)
Provenance:
Bishop W.C. White Collection.

Published:
H. Trubner, *The Far Eastern Collection*
(Toronto: ROM, 1968), p. 60 no. 74.

38. **Stem-cup**
Porcelain with bluish-white glaze.
Ht. 3-5/16" (8.4 cm.), diam. of mouth
3-5/16" (8.4 cm.), diam. of base.
1-9/16" (4 cm.)
921.21.2

T'ang Dynasty (618-906)
Provenance:
George Crofts Collection.

Published:
"West-East," ROMA *Bulletin*, No. 21
(Oct. 1953), no. 129a;
T. Dexel, *Die Formen chinesisches
Keramik* (Tubingen: Wasmuth, 1955),
Pl. 46c;
D. Rhodes, *Stoneware and Porcelain*
(New York: Chilton, 1959), Pl. 18;
T.A. Heinrich, *Art Treasures in the ROM*
(Toronto, 1963), p. 58;
H. Trubner, *The Far Eastern Collection*
(Toronto: ROM, 1968), p. 49 no. 56.

39. **Vase**
Ch'ing-pai ware, porcellaneous
stoneware; decoration incised and
carved under blue-white glaze.
Ht. 11½" (29.2 cm.)
925.25.27

Sun-Yüan Dynasty, 12th-13th
century.
Provenance:
George Crofts Collection.

Published:
J. Wirgin, "Sung Ceramic Designs,"
*Bulletin of the Museum of Far Eastern
Antiquities*, Stockholm, No. 42

(1970), p. 59, Pl. 22j.

40. **Vase**
Ch'ing-pai ware, porcelain; incised
and combed decoration under pale
bluish-white glaze.
Ht. 11-3/16" (28.4 cm.)
922.20.98

Yüan Dynasty, 13th-14th century.
Provenance:
George Crofts Collection. Reportedly
from Shun-te Fu, now Hsing-t'ai Hsien,
Hopei province.

Published:
A. Lane, "The Gaignières-Fonthill
Vase: A Chinese Porcelain of About
1300," *The Burlington Magazine*, CIII
(April 1961), p. 131, fig. 8;
T.A. Heinrich, *Art Treasures in the ROM*
(Toronto, 1963), p. 59;
H. Trubner, *The Far Eastern Collection*
(Toronto: ROM, 1968), p. 66 no. 82;
S. Lee and W.K. Ho, *Chinese Art Under
the Mongols* (Cleveland Museum of
Art, 1968), pp. 16-17, no. 100.

41. Śākyamuni Buddha

Ch'ing-pai ware, porcelain; greyish
white body covered with greenish-
white glaze.
Ht. 10½" (26.7 cm.), w. at base 8"
(20.3 cm.)
922.20.109

Yüan Dynasty, 13th-14th century.
Provenance:
George Crofts Collection. Reportedly
from Shen-te Fu (?), Honan province.

Published:
H. Trubner, "Two Examples of Ch'ing-
pai Porcelain in the Royal Ontario
Museum," *Archives of Asian Art*. Vol.
17 (1963), pp. 38-39 fig. 1;
S. Lee and W.K. Ho, *Chinese Art under
the Mongols* (Cleveland Museum of
Art, 1968), no. 28.

42. Bowl

Porcelain; decorated under bluish-white glaze, on the interior in raised slip, on the exterior with incised lines; base recessed and convex in depressed cone.
Ht. 4" (10.2 cm.), diam. at mouth 8-1/16" (20.5 cm.)
910.59.49

Ming Dynasty, early 15th century.

Published:
H. Trubner, *The Far Eastern Collection* (Toronto: ROM, 1968) p. 66 no. 81.

43. Plate

Porcelain decorated in underglaze blue; colour in "heaped and piled" effect, glaze with "orange peel" texture.
Ht. 2¾" (7 cm.), diam. 16⅛" (41 cm.)
962.256

Ming Dynasty, early 15th century.

Published:
H. Trubner, *The Far Eastern Collection* (Toronto: ROM, 1968), p. 67 no. 83.
Cf. J.A. Pope, *Chinese Porcelains from the Ardebil Shrine* (Washington: Freer Gallery of Art, 1956), Pls. 30-31;
Ming Blue-and-White from Swedish Collections (Stockholm: Museum of Far Eastern Antiquities, 1964), no. 20.

44. Covered Jar *(kuan)*

Porcelain decorated in underglaze blue; colour in "heaped and piled" effect, glaze with "orange peel" texture.
Ht. 13½" (34.25 cm.)
925.25.15

Ming Dynasty, Interregnum (1435-1465)
Provenance:
George Crofts Collection.

Published:
Sir Harry M. Garner, *Oriental Blue and White* (New York: Pitman, 1954), Pl. 23;
O-Bei shuzo Chugoku tōji zuroku (Chinese Ceramics in the West), ed. J.

Mayuyama (Tokyo: Mayuyama, 1960), Pl. 91;
A.M. Ferris, "An Early 15th Century Kuan in Toronto," *Oriental Art*, IX:2 (Summer 1963), p. 98;
H. Trubner, *The Far Eastern Collection* (Toronto: ROM, 1968), p. 67, no. 84.

45. Covered Box

Porcelain decorated in underglaze blue. Arabic inscriptions—on top, "Seek good penmanship for it is among the keys to good fortune"; on long sides, "The fool does not cause pleasure just as he does not serve friendship"; on short sides, "Wisdom is a possessor of arms." Six character Cheng-te mark on base.
Ht. 4½" (10.8 cm.), l. 10¼" (26 cm.), w. 7⅛" (15.6 cm.)
925.25.2

Ming Dynasty, Cheng-te period (1506-1521).
Provenance:
George Crofts Collection.

Published:
"West-East," ROMA *Bulletin,* No. 21 (Oct. 1953), pp. 34-35, no. 153; H.M. Garner, *Oriental Blue and White* (London: Faber, 1954), p. 28, Pl. 43A; H. Trubner, *The Far Eastern Collection* (Toronto: ROM, 1968), p. 68 no. 85. Cf. *Arts de l'Islam* (Paris: Orangerie, 1971), no. 112, for a similar container for ink palettes with identical top inscription in the Musée Guimet, Paris.

46. Jar (oviform *kuan*)
Porcelain decorated in underglaze
blue; painted in clear violet-blue
outlines and lighter washes. Six
character Chia-ching mark in
horizontal panel beneath lip.
Ht. 14¾" (37.46 cm.)
923.17.23

Ming Dynasty, Chia-ching period
(1522-1566)
Provenance:
George Crofts Collection.

47. Brush-Holder
Porcelain decorated in underglaze
blue; painted in "pencilled" style. Six
character Ch'eng-hua mark on base.
Ht. 5½" (13.9 cm.), diam. at mouth
3½" (8.9 cm.)
923.17.31

Ming—Ch'ing Dynasty, Transition,
17th century.
Provenance:
George Crofts Collection.

Published:
A.M.Ferris, "17th Century
Transitional Porcelains," *Oriental Art*,
xiv:3 (Autumn 1968), p. 187, fig. 7.

48. **Bottle-Vase**
Porcelain decorated in underglaze
blue; painted in outline and wash, as
well as "pencilled" style.
Ht. 9⅛" (23.3 cm.)
911.4.45

Ch'ing Dynasty, early K'ang-hsi
period, 1662-1683.

Published:
A.M.Ferris, "17th Century
Transitional Porcelains," *Oriental Art,*
xiv:3 (Autumn 1968), p. 190 fig.17.

49. **Jar** *(kuan)*
Porcelain decorated in underglaze
blue line and layers of wash.
Ht. 12¼" (31 cm.)
923.17.20

Ming—Ch'ing Dynasty, Transition,
17th century.
Provenance:
George Crofts Collection.

50. **Vase** (baluster shape)
Porcelain decorated in underglaze blue and overglaze enamels of *tou-ts'ai* type. Six character Ch'eng-hua mark on base.
Ht. 16⅝" (42.2 cm.)
911.4.32

Ch'ing Dynasty, K'ang-hsi period (1662-1722).
Published:
H. Trubner, *The Far Eastern Collection* (Toronto: ROM, 1968), p. 74 no. 96.

Bronze

The early Chinese bronzes in the ROM are closely associated with Bishop William C. White, who collected most of them in the 1920s and 1930s while he was active in Honan province. It was a time when Chinese art was receiving great public attention throughout the world, and during the 1930s Bishop White's lively notices about the growing collection of early Chinese art in Toronto appeared regularly in the international press and brought increased recognition to the ROM.

Both Bishop White and Dr. James M. Menzies, whose study collections of Bronze Age material came to the ROM in 1960, were fascinated by the technical perfection of early Chinese bronzes. For many years art historians believed that the intricate designs on Chinese Bronze Age objects could only have been cast by the *cire perdue*, or lost-wax, process. Both men, however, acquired fragments of the ceramic piece-moulds that were found at Shang Dynasty sites near An-yang, and realized that they were important evidence of the technique used by the bronze makers. Today scholars have accepted the fact that all of the earliest Chinese bronzes were made by the laborious and difficult piece-mould method. Only great familiarity with the properties of both the ceramics from which the moulds were made, and the metal that was cast in them, could have resulted in the production in this manner of bronze vessels of a quality unexcelled in the ancient world.

When the collecting of bronzes in the West began early in this century, dating of material made earlier than the Han Dynasty was extremely difficult. Relative dating within the Shang Dynasty, the period when bronze was first used, has remained difficult until the last few years. Chinese reports on a number of Shang sites have now clarified the stylistic sequence. Information contained in recent archaeological reports from China has frequently enhanced our understanding of the ROM's bronzes. In 1947 Bishop White acquired for the ROM a puzzling group of vessels (see No. 51). Compared with Shang vessels of more familiar types—heavy and substantial, with decoration of stylized animal elements against fine spiral grounds—these pieces were small, light, and sparsely decorated. Bishop White realized that, while they were suggestive of Shang style, they were also distinctive, and decided they must be later pieces in a diluted Shang tradition. Modern archaeology has established that his reasoning was right although his dating was too modest, for pieces of this type are now known to have been made very early, when Shang style was just beginning its development, rather than later.

The largest and most impressive group of bronzes associated with Bishop White is the material said to have come from large tombs at Chin-ts'un, near Lo-yang, in Honan province. It represents the end of the Bronze Age, a period nearly a thousand years removed from that of the vessels mentioned above.

Musical instruments, mirrors (see No. 67), figures that may have supported lamps (see No. 75), and bronze fittings inlaid with precious metals (see Nos. 68-74), all provide insight into the taste of the ruling class of the time.

Both Bishop White and Dr. Menzies were keenly interested in the bronzes as historical documents as well as art objects. Bishop White endeavoured to collect bronzes that were associated and formed groups. Dr. Menzies studied the inscriptions on the bronzes and attempted to relate them to what was known of Shang history and genealogy. Dr. Menzies' personal collection of Shang Dynasty bronze study objects, many of them too broken or fragmentary for display, has also provided the ROM with an important body of material on which to base research on the history of technology in ancient China.

Helen E. Fernald, who succeeded Bishop White as Keeper of the Far Eastern Department, respected the strength of the Chinese bronze collection, but also saw one area of weakness in it. While the material acquired earlier was rich and varied, relatively few pieces demonstrated the full power of the finest Shang and early Chou Dynasty art. In the early 1950s, at the beginning of a period of soaring prices that would make significant collecting in this field almost impossible, she interested a Toronto donor in a group of six bronze vessels of exceptional quality. Four of the pieces which made up the subsequent gift are illustrated (see Nos. 52-53, 57 & 59). They, and the *fang-i* acquired soon after (see No. 54), are today recognized as being among the finest vessels of their date in any western collection.

Barbara Stephen

80

51. **Tripod Wine Vessel** *(chia)*
Bronze; traces of fibrous material on sides and handle.
Ht. 9½" (24.1 cm.)
947.33.10

Shang Dynasty, 14th–13th century B.C.
Provenance:
Bishop W.C. White Collection
Gift of the Flavelle Foundation in memory of Sir Joseph Flavelle.
Reportedly found at the village of Tung-shih-ho, east of Hui Hsien, Honan province, with other objects of the "Prince Kung" group.

Published:
Illustrated London News, Dec. 20, 1947, p. 701 fig. 8;
W.C. White, *Bronze Culture of Ancient China* (Toronto: Univ. Press, 1956), Pl. LXXXI;
B. Stephen, "Early Chinese Bronzes in the Royal Ontario Museum" *Oriental Art*, Vol. VIII (1962), p. 64 no. 5.
Cf. M. Loehr, *Ritual Vessels of Bronze Age China* (New York: Asia Society, 1968), no. 8, a *chia* in the Sackler Collections;
K'ao-ku hsüeh-pao, No. 15 (1957), Pl. 3:3, a *chia* with somewhat more developed decoration found at Cheng-chou, Honan province;
Hui Hsien fa-chüeh pao-kao (Peking: K'o-hsueh, 1956), Pl. 14:3, a *chia* with similar decoration and almost identical form excavated at Liu-li-ko, Hui Hsien, Honan province.

52. **Wine Vessel** *(tsun)*
Bronze.
Ht. 13¾" (34.9 cm.)
954.136.2

Shang Dynasty, An-yang period, 13th century.
Purchased with funds from the Reuben Wells Leonard Bequest.

Published:
Tch'ou To-yi, *Bronze Antiques de la Chine appartenant à C.T. Loo et Cie* (Paris & Brussels: G. van Oest, 1924), Pl. 25a;
S. Umehara, *Shina kodō seikwa* (Osaka: Yamanaka, 1933), Pl. 33;
B. Karlgren, "New Studies on Chinese Bronzes," *Bulletin of the Museum of Far Eastern Antiquities*, Stockholm, No. 9 (1937), Pl. LI, no. 759;
"Marginalia on Some Bronze Albums: II," *Ibid.*, No. 32 (1960), Pl. 25a;
H.E. Fernald, "Six Bronze Vessels from China," ROMA *Bulletin*, No. 23 (May 1955), fig. 1;
H. Trubner, *The Far Eastern Collection* (Toronto: ROM, 1968), p. 13 no. 6.
Cf. *K'ao-ku hsüeh-pao*, No. 3 (1948–49), Pl. VI:2, a comparable *tsun* excavated from Hsiao-t'un, An-yang, Honan province; No. 15 (1957), Pl. 3:1, a *tsun* excavated at Pai-chia-chuang, Cheng-chou, Honan.

53. **Wine Jar** *(hu)*
Bronze; one character inscription on
interior below rim.
Ht. 15⅜" (39 cm.)
954.136.3

Shang Dynasty, An-yang period, *c.*
1300-1028 B.C.
Purchased with funds from the
Reuben Wells Leonard Bequest.

Published: .
H.E. Fernald, "Six Bronze Vessels from
China," ROMA *Bulletin,* No. 23 (1955),
fig. 3;
T.A. Heinrich, *Art Treasures in the* ROM
(Toronto, 1963), p. 31;
H. Trubner, *The Far Eastern Collection*
(Toronto: ROM, 1968), p. 25 no. 16.
Cf. J.A. Pope et al., *The Freer Chinese
Bronzes,* Vol. I (Washington: Freer
Gallery of Art, 1967), Pl. 5, no. 5, a *hu*
with similar decoration.

55. **Covered Water Vessel** *(kuang)*
Bronze; decoration includes the head of a Muntjac deer on the lid, and the figure of an elephant with upraised trunk on either side.
L. 9-7/16" (24 cm.)
933.12.52

Shang Dynasty, An-yang period, *c.* 1300-1028 B.C.
Provenance:
Bishop W.C. White Collection.
Reportedly discovered near Ta-ssu-k'ung-ts'un, An-yang, Honan province, with other objects from the "Elephant Tomb" group.

Published:
Illustrated London News, May 18, 1935, Pl.IV no. 2, p. 888 fig. 4, p. 889 fig. 12;
C. Hentze, *Bronzegerät, Kultbauten, Religion im ältesten China der Shang-zeit* (Antwerp: de Sikkel, 1951), Pls. LXIV-LXV;
W.C. White, *Bronze Culture of Ancient China* (Toronto: Univ. Press, 1956), Pl.V;
J. LeRoy Davidson, "The Riddle of the Bottle Horn," *Artibus Asiae*, Vol. XXII (1959), fig. 7 facing p. 21;
H. Trubner, *The Far Eastern Collection* (Toronto: ROM, 1968), p. 1 no. 1.
Cf. *Selected Specimens of the Chinese Bronze Collection in the Hakkaku Art Museum* (Kobe: Hakutsuru Hakubutsukan (1951), no. 8, a *kuang* with elephant head relief on the cover, reportedly found with the "Elephant Tomb" group, now in the Hakutsuru Museum near Kobe.

56. **Tripod Wine Cup** *(chüeh)*
Bronze; black substance inlaid to recessed parts of design; one character inscription under handle.
Ht. 8-7/16" (21.5 cm.)
947.31.4

Shang Dynasty, An-yang period, *c.* 12th century B.C.
Provenance:
Bishop W.C. White Collection.

Published:
Liang Shang-ch'un, ed., *Yen-k'u chi-chin t'u-lu* (Peking: Ts'ai-hua, 1944), Vol. I, Pl. 26;
W. C. White, "A Shang Libation Cup," *Oriental Art*, III:2 (1950), pp. 48-49;
S. Umehara, *Inkyo* (Tokyo: Asahi Shinbun, 1964), Pl. LXXVI;
H.Y. Shih, "The Study of Chinese Bronzes as Art and Craft," *World Archaeology*, III:3 (Feb. 1972), Pl. 12.
Cf. S.H. Hansford, *The Seligman Collection of Oriental Art* (London: Arts Council, 1957), Pl.IV, no. A5.

57. Tripod Food Vessel *(ting)*
Bronze; black substance inlaid in
recessed parts of design; five
character inscription on interior side.
Ht. 13⅜" (33.9 cm.)
954.136.1

Shang Dynasty, An-yang period,
12th-11th century B.C
Purchased with funds from the
Reuben Wells Leonard Bequest.

Published:
P. Ackerman, *Ritual Bronzes of
Ancient China* (New York: 1945), Pl.
15;
H.E. Fernald, "Six Bronze Vessels from
China," ROMA *Bulletin,* No. 23 (1955),
fig. 2;
T.A. Heinrich, *Art Treasures in the* ROM
(Toronto, 1963), p. 31;
H. Trubner, *The Far Eastern Collection*
(Toronto: ROM, 1968), p. 25 no. 17.

59. Covered Wine Jar with Swing Handle *(yu)*
Bronze; two three-character inscriptions, inside cover and on interior bottom.
Ht. 13¾" (34.9 cm.)
954.136.5

Early Western Chou Dynasty, 11th-10th century B.C.
Purchased with funds from the Reuben Wells Leonard Bequest.

Published:
H.E. Fernald, "Six Bronze Vessels from China," ROMA *Bulletin,* No. 23 (1955), fig. 4;
H. Trubner, *The Far Eastern Collection* (Toronto: ROM, 1968), p. 22 no. 11.
Cf. B. Karlgren, *A Catalogue of the Chinese Bronzes in the Alfred F. Pillsbury Collection* (Minneapolis Institute of Arts, 1952), Pl. 26, no. 18;
S. Umehara, *Nihon shūcho Shina kodō seikwa,* Vol. I (Osaka: Yamanaka, 1959), Pl. XLIX, a similar *yu* in the Neiraku Art Museum, Nara;
K'ao Ku, 1963 no. 4, p. 225 fig. 1 rt., a similar *yu* from I-ch'eng Hsien, Shansi province.

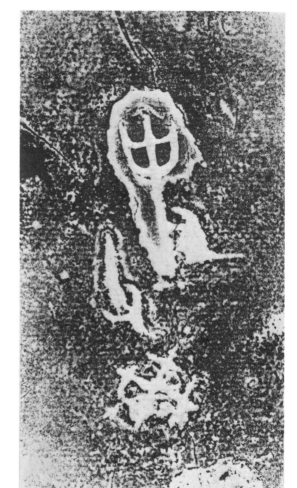

60. Square Vessel
Bronze; two bands below rim with inlaid designs in copper, gold, malachite and turquoise.
Ht. 7-13/16" (19.8 cm.)
933.12.54

Eastern Chou Dynasty, late 6th-early 5th century B.C
Provenance:
Bishop W.C. White Collection.
Reportedly from Chin-ts'un, Honan province.

Published:
Illustrated London News, October 28, 1933, p. 701 fig. 7;
W.C. White, *Tombs of Old Lo-yang* (Shanghai: Kelly & Walsh, 1934), Pl.CXIII;
J.G. Andersson, "The Goldsmith in Ancient China," *Bulletin of the Museum of Far Eastern Art*, Stockholm, No. 7 (1934), Pls.II & III;
S. Umehara, *Rakuyō Kinson kobo shūei* (Kyoto: Kobayashi, 1937), App. Pl.VIII;
B. Karlgren, "Huai and Han," *Bulletin of the Museum of Far Eastern Art*, Stockholm, No. 13 (1941), Pl. 6:6;
L. Bachhofer, *A Short History of Chinese Art* (New York: Pantheon, 1946), p. 47 fig.XII;
H. Trubner, *The Far Eastern Collection* (Toronto: ROM, 1968), p. 27 no. 20.
Cf. *Shou Hsien Ts'ai hou mu ch'u-t'u i-wu* (Peking: K'o-hsüeh, 1956), Pl. 14:3, a vessel of similar shape excavated from the tomb of the

Marquis of Ts'ai at Shou Hsien, Anhui province.

61. Covered Tripod Food Vessel
Bronze; details of design, such as eyes
of supporting figures, inset with small
glass beads.
L. 7⅞" (20 cm.)
932.16.71

Eastern Chou Dynasty, 6th-5th
century B.C.
Provenance:
Bishop W.C. White Collection.
Reportedly from Chin-ts'un, Honan
province.

Published:
Illustrated London News, October 28,
1933, p. 701 fig. 3;
W.C. White, *Tombs of Old Lo-yang*
(Shanghai: Kelly & Walsh, 1934),
Frontispiece & Pl.c;
S. Umehara, *Rakuyō Kinson kobo
shūei* (Kyoto: Kobayashi, 1937), Pl.vi;
The Art of Eastern Chou (New York:
Chinese Art Society of America,
1962), no. 40;
H. Trubner, *The Far Eastern Collection*
(Toronto: ROM, 1968), p. 28 no. 21.
Cf. B. Karlgren, *The Pillsbury
Collection of Chinese Bronzes*
(Minneapolis Institute of Arts, 1952),
Pl. 70, no. 50, an almost identical
vessel;
Ku Kung t'ung-ch'i t'u-lu, (Taipei:
Chung-hua ts'ung-shu wei-yüan hui,
1948), Vol.II, Pl. 188 bottom, a vessel
in the National Central Museum
collection, of which a line drawing
was published in *Hsi-ch'ing hsü-chien
i-pien* (Peking: Ku-wu ch'en-lieh so,
1931), Vol.II fasc. 17, p. 3.

**62. Covered Cylindrical Box with
Swing Handle** *(lien)*
Bronze.
Ht. 7-7/16" (19.1 cm.)
932.16.44

Han Dynasty (206 B.C.-A.D. 220).
Provenance:
Bishop W.C. White Collection.

Published:
H. Trubner, *The Far Eastern Collection*
(Toronto: ROM, 1968), p. 33 no. 32.
Cf. *Guide Book* (Seoul: National
Museum of Korea, 1964), p. 31 no.
25, a very similar *lien* with more
complex handle, excavated from a site
associated with the Han Dynasty
colony at Lo-lang in northern Korea;
Ch'ang-sha fa-chüeh pao-kao
(Peking: Academy of Science, 1957),
Pl. 64:3, a former Han Dynasty *lien*
with mask and ring handles, from a
tomb at Ch'ang-sha, Hunan province.

63. **Censer with Hill-Cover** *(po-shan-lu)*
Bronze.
Ht. 7-1/16" (18 cm.)
922.20.93

Former Han Dynasty (206 B.C.-A.D. 8).
Provenance:
George Crofts Collection.

Published:
H. Trubner, *The Arts of the Han Dynasty* (New York: Chinese Art Society of America, 1961), no. 43; *The Far Eastern Collection* (Toronto: ROM, 1968), p. 32 no. 31.
Cf. *K'ao-ku hsüeh-pao*, No. 32 (1963), Pl.VI:8-9, two ceramic *po-shan-lu* excavated from the western suburbs of Lo-yang, Honan province; *Wen Wu*, 1972 no. 1, Pl. 4, p. 12, a *po-shan-lu* discovered in a 2nd century B.C. tomb at Man-ch'eng, Hopei province.

64. Phoenix Lamp

Bronze; fifty-three character inscription on side of dish, giving its date of manufacture in 28 B.C. by artisans in the imperial workshops for an official of the Central Palace.
Ht. 7½" (18.9 cm.)
933.12.124

Former Han Dynasty, 28 B.C.
Provenance:
Bishop W.C. White Collection.

Published: *Illustrated London News*, April 4, 1936, Pl. I;
M.R. Allen, "Early Chinese Lamps," *Oriental Art*, II:4 (1950), p. 139 no. 16.
Cf. *K'ao Ku*, 1972 no. 1, Pl. 6:1, a phoenix lamp of similar style; pp. 11-12 figs. 6-8, Pl. 7:1, comparable inscriptions on other bronze vessels; all from a 2nd century B.C. tomb at Man-ch'eng, Hopei province.

65. **Bell** *(chung)*
Bronze; remains of clay casting core
inside handle.
Ht. 22¼" (56.5 cm.)
931.13.165

Early Western Chou Dynasty, 10th
century B.C.
Provenance:
Bishop W.C. White Collection.
Reportedly from the Hang-chou region,
Chechiang province.

Published:
K'ao-ku hsüeh-pao, No. 13 (1956), Pl.
12:3 following p. 128.
Cf. E. von Erdberg Consten, *Das Alte
China* (Stuttgart: Gustav Kilpper
Verlag, 1958), Pl. 40, for a similar bell
in the Portland Art Museum;
Wen Wu, 1959 no. 10, p. 33 fig. 3, a
very similar bell collected in Shang-
hai, Kiangsu province;
Ibid., 1960 no. 7, p. 49, another bell
of the same general type found at
Ch'ang-hsing, Chechiang province.

66. Dagger-Axe (ko)
Bronze; turquoise inlay on butt.
L. 15-13/16" (40.2 cm.)
934.17.43

Shang Dynasty, An-yang period, c.
1300-1028 B.C.
Provenance:
Bishop W.C. White Collection.
Reportedly discovered near Ta-ssu-
k'ung-ts'un, An-yang, Honan province,
with other objects from the
"Elephant Tomb" group.

Published:
Illustrated London News, May 18,
1935, p. IV no. 6;
W.C. White, *Bronze Culture of Ancient
China* (Toronto: Univ. Press, 1956),
Pl. VI b, p. 201 fig. 2.
Cf. Li Chi, *The Beginnings of Chinese
Civilization* (Seattle: Univ. of
Washington Press, 1957), Pl. XVI, no.
14, a similar large dagger-axe with
down-curved butt inlaid with
turquoise, and no. 15, another
example of the same type with jade
blade; both from Hsiao-t'un, An-yang,
Honan province.

67. Square Mirror
Bronze; some turquoise inlay in
decoration.
W. 3-9/16" (9.1 cm.)
932.16.107

Eastern Chou Dynasty, 5th century B.C.
Provenance:
Bishop W.C. White Collection.
Reportedly from Chin-ts'un, Honan
province.

Published:
W.C. White, *Tombs of Old Lo-yang*
(Shanghai: Kelly & Walsh, 1934), Pl. LI
no. 128;
S. Umehara, *Kan izen no kokyō no
kenkyū* (Kyoto: Tōhō bunka, 1935),
fig. 2 no. 7; *Rakuyō kinson kobo shūei*
(Kyoto: Kobayashi, 1937), Pl. L
A. Salmony, "On Early Chinese
Mirrors," *Art in America,* Vol. 30
(1942), p. 196 fig. 5;
The Art of Eastern Chou (New York:
Chinese Art Society of America,
1962), no. 57;
E. Bunker, "A Little Known Type of
Eastern Han Mirror," *Archives of the
Chinese Art Society,* Vol. XXVII (1963),
p. 40;
D. Dohrenwend, "The Early Chinese
Mirror," *Artibus Asiae,* Vol. XXVII: 1/2
(1964), Pl. I, fig. 1D;
H. Trubner, *The Far Eastern Collection*
(Toronto: ROM, 1968), p. 26 no. 19.
Cf. S. Umehara, *Kan izen no kokyō no
kenkyū,* Pl. 35, fig. 1, and p. 37 fig. 20;
A. Salmony, "Chinese Metal Mirrors,"
Hobbies, Vol. 25 (1945), p. 97 fig. 1.

68. Handle
Bronze; decoration inlaid with gold
and silver wire.
L. 3⅜" (8.6 cm.)
931.13.72

Eastern Chou Dynasty, 4th-3rd
century B.C.
Provenance:
Bishop W.C. White Collection.
Reportedly from Chin-ts'un, Honan
province.

Published:
W.C. White, *Tombs of Old Lo-yang*
(Shanghai: Kelly & Walsh, 1934), Pl. v,
no. 007C.
Cf. S. Umehara, *Rakuyō kinson kobo
shūei* (Kyoto: Tōhō bunka, 1937), P. LXV

69. Animal-Head Finial
Bronze; decoration inlaid with gold
and silver wire.
L. 2⅞" (7.3 cm.)
931.13.71

Eastern Chou Dynasty, 4th-3rd
century B.C.
Provenance:
Bishop W.C. White Collection.
Reportedly from Chin-ts'un, Honan
province.

Published:
W.C. White, *Tombs of Old Lo-yang*
(Shanghai: Kelly & Walsh, 1934), Pl. vi,
no. 015A;
The Art of Eastern Chou (New York:
Chinese Art Society of America,
1962), no. 35;

H. Trubner, *The Far Eastern Collection*
(Toronto: ROM, 1968), p. 30 no. 25, left.
Cf. S. Umehara, *Rakuyō kinson kobo
shūei* (Kyoto: Tōhō bunka, 1937),
Pl. LXIII: 1.

70. Finial or Axle-Cap

Bronze; decoration inlaid with gold
and silver sheet and wire; end inset
with white and dark blue glass.
L. 4⅛" (10.5 cm.)
931.13.9

Eastern Chou Dynasty, 4th-3rd
century B.C.
Provenance:
Bishop W.C. White Collection.
Reportedly from Chin-ts'un, Honan
province.

Published:
W.C. White, *Tombs of Old Lo-yang*
(Shanghai: Kelly & Walsh, 1934), Pl.
VI, no. 014B;
H. Trubner, *The Far Eastern Collection*
(Toronto: ROM, 1968), p. 31 no. 27.
Cf. S. Umehara, *Rakuyō kinson kobo
shūei* (Kyoto: Tōhō bunka, 1937), Pl.
LXIII:3-4.

71. Finial

Bronze; decoration inlaid with gold
and silver wire.
L. 2-7/16" (6.1 cm.)
931.13.68

Eastern Chou Dynasty, 4th-3rd
century B.C.
Provenance:
Bishop W.C. White Collection.
Reportedly from Chin-ts'un, Honan
province.

Published:
W.C. White, *Tombs of Old Lo-yang*
(Shanghai: Kelly & Walsh, 1934), Pls.

VI-VII, no. 013A.

72. Finial

Bronze; decoration inlaid with gold
and silver wire.
L. 2-9/16" (6.5 cm.)
929.11.140

Eastern Chou Dynasty, 4th-3rd
century B.C.
Provenance:
Bishop W.C. White Collection.
Reportedly from Chin-ts'un, Honan
province.

Published:
W.C. White, *Tombs of Old Lo-yang*
(Shanghai: Kelly & Walsh, 1934), Pl. IV,
no. 011A.
H. Trubner, *The Far Eastern Collection*
(Toronto: ROM, 1968), p. 30 no. 26 left.

73. **Ring**
Bronze; decoration inlaid with gold
and silver wire.
Diam. 4-3/16" (10.5 cm.)
931.13.65

Eastern Chou Dynasty, 4th-3rd
century B.C.
Provenance:
Bishop W.C. White Collection.
Reportedly from Chin-ts'un, Honan
province.

Published:
W.C. White, *Tombs of Old Lo-yang*,
(Shanghai: Kelly & Walsh, 1934), Pl.
v, no. 010A.

74. Circular Fitting
Gilt bronze; centre inset with white
and dark blue glass.
Diam. 2⅝" (6.1 cm.)
930.21.2A

Eastern Chou Dynasty, 4th-3rd
century B.C.
Provenance:
Bishop W.C. White Collection.
Reportedly from Chin-ts'un, Honan
province.

Published:
W.C. White, *Tombs of Old Lo-yang*
(Shanghai: Kelly & Walsh, 1934),
Pl.CLIII, no. 401.

Tomb Figurines

With the exception of a few examples, acquired through Bishop William C. White and Dr. James M. Menzies, or by purchase from other sources, the vast collection of Chinese tomb figurines was gathered by Mr. George Crofts. At the time of his greatest activity on behalf of the Museum, in the 1920s, extensive construction for the Lung-hai Railway was revealing hundreds of burials in the path of this east to west line in north China. Chinese were reluctant to remove objects from tombs, but economic conditions through the Yellow River valley ("China's sorrow" with its recurrent floods and famines) often forced labourers to supplement their meagre incomes by sale of such artifacts. Seen in the light of contemporary market values, tomb figurines were sold fifty years ago for pathetic sums—often only 10 Mexican silver dollars for a cartload.

The earliest remaining examples of these substitutes for real human or animal sacrifices are made of bronze. Half a dozen specimens (see No. 75) are housed in the ROM; more than have emerged in Chinese excavations of the past twenty-five years.

Most tomb figurines are of clay, a material both cheaper and more easily worked. Death cults were most popular during the Han and T'ang dynasties, so those periods produced the largest quantity and variety of burial materials. We have especially good representation in tomb figurines from the 2nd and 3rd centuries, and again the 7th century. The selection published here was chosen to demonstrate the range of sculptural concepts and technical skills which aroused the admiration leading to their acquisition for Toronto. We have also focused upon types less often seen in other collections and museums.

The Museum collection is weaker in provincial examples, having mainly come from China's so-called "nuclear area" in the northern provinces of Honan and Shansi. Thus, we have no wood figurines of the type produced in Kwantung province in China's extreme south-east during the Han Dynasty. Nor do we have more than one possible specimen from Szechwan province to the south-west. Recognition of such regional products has emerged only in the last two decades with the results of numerous excavations in the People's Republic of China. Those anxious to pursue their understanding of this area in Chinese art must find opportunity to visit the National Historical Museum in Peking. In the meantime, Toronto provides a strong basis for grasp of principal types and stylistic variations.

Hsio-Yen Shih

77. Female Attendant

Tomb figurine, earthenware cast in
two-part moulds with considerable
carved finishing; pale grey body.
Ht. 17½" (44.5 cm.)
920.1.9

Later Han Dynasty, A.D. 2nd century.
Provenance:
George Crofts Collection.
Reportedly from Lu-an Fu, now
Ch'ang-chih Hsien, Shansi province.

Published:
H.E. Fernald, "An Early Type of
Chinese Burial Figure," ROMA *Bulletin*,
No. 24 (Dec. 1956), pp. 28-31, Pl.
13 c.

78. Gymnasts

Tomb figurines, earthenware cast in
four-part moulds with manipulation of
the "leather" clay after joining
sections; grey body covered with
white ground, traces of orange-red
pigment. Ht. 4" (10.3 cm.)—4¾"
(11.9 cm.)
923.1.29-.30

Former Han Dynasty (206 B.C. - A.D. 8).
Provenance:
George Crofts Collection.

Reportedly from Lao-yang (*sic*,
Lo-yang?) Hsien, Honan province.

Published:
E. Schafer, *Ancient China* (New York:
Time-Life, 1967), p.181, where they
are erroneously placed in a section on
the T'ang Dynasty.

79. Wrestler (?)

Tomb figurine, earthenware modelled and carved; hard dark grey body covered with white ground, traces of flesh-coloured pigment on unclothed parts and of red pigment at belt and trouser-leg borders. Ht. 5⅜" (13.7 cm.)
960.238.32

Later Han Dynasty (A.D. 25-220).
Provenance:
Dr. James M. Menzies Collection. Reportedly excavated on the north bank of the Chang River, near An-yang, Honan province, from a burial of the Northern Chou Dynasty (578-581).
Cf. *Ch'üan-kuo chi-pen chien-she kung-ch'eng chung ch'u-t'u wen-wu tsan-lan t'u-lu* (Peking: Chung-kuo ku-tien i-shu, 1956), Pls. 69-70, for finds of tomb figurines from a Northern Chou tomb excavated at Ti-chang-wan, Hsien-yang, Shensi province, which are stylistically related to Sui or early T'ang Dynasty examples.

80. Labourer

Tomb figurine, earthenware cast in two-part moulds in exact position; very hard light grey body with a vitrified surface both silvery and granular in appearance. Ht. 4¼" (10.9 cm.)
920.1.197

Later Han Dynasty (A.D. 25-220).
Provenance:
George Crofts Collection.

81. Entertainers

Tomb figurines, earthenware
modelled around cone-shaped spike;
pinkish body covered with green
glaze. Ht. 3" (9 cm.)—3¾" (9.9 cm.)
921.21.118-.119

Later Han Dynasty (A.D. 25-220).
Provenance:
George Crofts Collection.

82. Female Servant

Tomb figurine, earthenware with head
cast in two-part moulds and body
wheel-turned with modelled details;
hard dark grey body with traces of
white ground and red pigment. Ht. 4"
(10.3 cm.)
923.10.5

Six Dynasties period, late 3rd-late 5th
century.
Provenance:
George Crofts Collection.
Cf. *K'ao-ku hsüeh-pao*, 1957 no. 1,
after p. 186, Pl. 3:4 and 7; and *K'ao
Ku*, 1959 no. 11, p. 606, Pl. 4:5; for
wheel-turned figurines from Western
Chin Dynasty tombs excavated in the
western suburbs of Lo-yang, Honan
province, including one with an
epitaph stone dated to A.D. 287.

84. Warrior Attendant
Tomb figurine, earthenware cast in two-part moulds with head separate and inserted to socket in body; coarse grey body with traces of white ground and red pigment.
Ht. 24½" (62.2 cm.)
920.1.52

Northern Ch'i Dynasty, third quarter of 6th century.
Provenance:
George Crofts Collection.
Cf. T. Nagahiro, *The Representational Art of the Six Dynasties Period* (Tokyo: Bijutsu shuppan-sha, 1969), Pls. 45-56, for close stylistic similarities in reliefs on the stone funeral bed at the William Rockhill Nelson Gallery of Art in Kansas City.

85. Male Attendant
Tomb figurine, earthenware with head cast in two-part moulds and inserted to socket in body pressed from single mould; coarse warm brown body except for head of finer grey clay. Ht. 32" (81.4 cm.)
918.2.12

Northern Ch'i Dynasty, third quarter of 6th century.
Provenance:
George Crofts Collection.
Cf. *K'ao-ku t'ung-hsün*, 1957, no. 3, Pls. 12-13, for figurines from the Feng family cemetary at Ching Hsien, Hopei province, placed as Northern Ch'i or Sui and with comparable features.

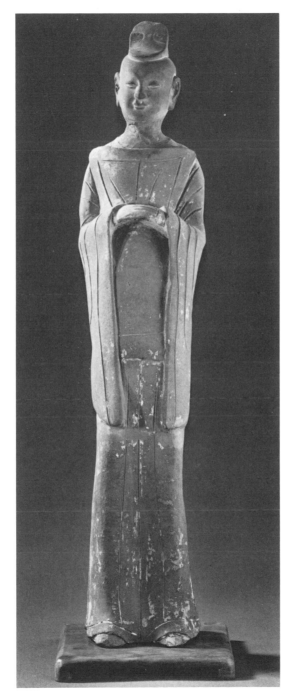

86. Spirit Guardians

Tomb figurines, earthenware cast in four-part moulds. Example with curling beard has iron armatures inserted in front legs before firing; hard dark grey body covered with white ground, flesh-coloured pigment on face and traces of green pigment analyzed as malachite on front leg feathers. Ht. 9¾" (24.9 cm.)
920.5.62
Example with helmet and mane has modelled legs and wings added; blue-grey body. Ht. 9½" (24.2 cm.)
920.5.63

Northern Ch'i-Sui Dynasty, later 6th century.
Provenance:
George Crofts Collection.
Cf. *Wen Wu*, 1964, no. 12, p. 68, for a female figurine discovered at Wei-li-ts'un, Huai-jou Hsien near Peking, Hopei province, with a brick inscribed to A.D. 571, which is similar in manufacture.

88. Female Attendants

Tomb figurines, earthenware modelled around iron armatures; grey body with remains of fired white slip. Ht. 12" (30.5 cm.)—13" (33.1 cm.)
921.1.19 and .21

Sui Dynasty (581-618).
Provenance:
George Crofts Collection.
Cf. *K'ao Ku*, 1959, no. 10, pp. 541-545, fig. 2, Pls. 10-11, for figurines of female musicians and servants dressed in similar costume found in the burial of a general, Chang Sheng, north of An-yang, Honan province, and dated by an epitaph stone to A.D. 595.

89. Nurse with Baby

Tomb figurine, earthenware cast in two-part moulds; hard dark grey body with traces of white ground and details in maroon-red analyzed as haematite, black and flesh-coloured pigments fired into slip. Ht. 5" (12.8 cm.)
920.1.34

Sui Dynasty (581-618).
Provenance:
George Crofts Collection.

90. Male Servant
Tomb figurine, earthenware cast in two-part moulds; medium hard white body with traces of surface details in black, red and flesh-coloured pigments. Ht. 5⅛" (13.1 cm.)
918.21.173

T'ang Dynasty, 7th century.
Provenance:
George Crofts Collection.

91. Equestrian
Tomb figurine, earthenware cast in four-part moulds for horse and two-part moulds for rider's head and torso, with details separately moulded or modelled and applied; soft buff body covered with originally white glaze now deteriorated to granular beige patches; painted details in black and red pigments fired into glaze. Ht. 17" (43.3 cm.)
923.24.126

Sui Dynasty, early 7th century.
Provenance:
George Crofts Collection.

92. Warrior Attendant
Tomb figurine, earthenware cast in two-part moulds with beard applied before glazing; soft fine white outer body lined with harder pinkish clay, milky white glaze minutely crazed but now decomposed, traces of black and red overglaze pigments. Ht. 19-4/5" (50.5 cm.)
921.21.6

Late Sui-early T'ang Dynasty, early 7th century.
Provenance:
George Crofts Collection.

Published:
E. Schafer, *Ancient China* (New York: Time-Life, 1967), p. 176.

NA-2938

93. Dancers or Mourners

Tomb figurines, earthenware cast in two-part moulds with arms modelled and added; very hard pale grey vitreous body covered with white ground under thin milky glaze tinged with light green, traces of black pigment fused in glaze for hair, and red pigments on scarf and ribbons. Ht. 7¾" (19.8 cm.)
921.21.104 and .105

T'ang Dynasty, 7th century.
Provenance:
George Crofts Collection.

94. Female and Male Attendants

Tomb figurines, earthenware rough-moulded then modelled in "leather" stage; body ranging from hard grey to soft buff, possibly fired with colouring slip. Ht. 12" (30.5 cm.)—10" (25.5 cm.)
957.217.2-.3

T'ang Dynasty, 7th century.
Reportedly from Ch'ang-sha, Hunan province.
Cf. *K'ao Ku*, 1958, no. 3, pp. 22-26, Pl. 4, for similar figures found in a tomb at Huang-t'u-ling, Ch'ang-sha, Hunan province.

95. Foreigner on Camel
Tomb figurine, earthenware cast in four-part moulds for camel's head and body, modelled for the rest; soft reddish body partially glazed over white ground analyzed as quartz; olive-green on figure and pack from lead glaze, amber with greenish tinge on camel analyzed as lead with traces of aluminium.
Ht. 19" (48.4 cm.), l. 15½" (39 cm.)
920.1.74

T'ang Dynasty, 7th century.
Provenance:
George Crofts Collection.
Cf. *K'ao Ku*, 1958, no. 1, p. 44, Pl. 9, for a comparable but stylistically more mature group found in the tomb of Tu-ku Ssu-ching, who was buried in A.D. 709 at what is now the eastern suburb of Hsi-an, Shensi province.

96. Horse
Tomb figurine, earthenware cast in four-part moulds for main form with details modelled and added; dark grey body covered with fired-on red pigment, harness details painted in black pigment and fired into red, saddle covered with white slip showing traces of green pigment; much incising and combing of clay.
Ht. 18¾" (47.7 cm.), l. 20" (50.9 cm.)
940.24.1

T'ang Dynasty, later 7th century.
Cf. O. Sirén, *A History of Early Chinese Art:* Sculpture (London: Ernest Benn, 1930), Pl. 97B, for a similar example in the Nedzu Museum, Tokyo.

97. Brahma Bull

Tomb figurine, earthenware cast in four-part moulds joined at neck; very hard off-white body covered with pale straw-coloured glaze showing brown flecks and greenish dapples through high firing of iron impurities. Ht. 8½" (21.7 cm.), l. 10" (25.5 cm.)
920.1.101

T'ang Dynasty, early 8th century.
Provenance:
George Crofts Collection.
Cf. *Wen Wu*, 1964, no. 1, p. 21 fig. 22, for a comparable animal model from the tomb of the Princess Yung-t'ai, buried in A.D. 706, at Ch'ien Hsien about 76.5 km. west of Hsi-an, Shensi province.

Sculptures

Despite Dr. Charles T. Currelly's enthusiasm for sculpture, and his urgings of Mr. George Crofts to purchase in this field, early acquisitions tended to be primarily in the later periods of Chinese sculptural development. Western criteria for judgment, based as they were then upon plastic principles formulated in the Greek and Roman ideal, found sympathetic echoes in China only when realistic representation had gained ground in the aesthetics of the Sung and Yüan dynasties.

Of the many wood images in the Museum's Chinese collections, the majority from Buddhist and Taoist temples in the Shansi-Shensi province areas, and ranging in date from the 12th through 19th centuries, about ten are of notable aesthetic or historical interest (see No. 112).

Rarer specimens are the marble monk (see No. 110) and the three-colour glazed earthenware *Lohan* (see No. 111). Both demonstrate an understanding of material and technical virtuosity, combined with a remarkable evocation of individual personality, which are readily appreciated in both East and West.

The Museum also has perhaps the best collection of Ming Dynasty cast-iron sculptures (see No. 113) in the western world, or outside of China.

The efforts of recent curators have been to provide material for the study of early sculptural history in China. Miss Helen E. Fernald and Mr. Henry Trubner both searched for Six Dynasties and T'ang Dynasty works of quality, and yet within our limited means. We now have representative examples in stone and gilt-bronze, both reliefs and carving in the round, monumental as well as small scaled.

There can be nothing in a museum to replace experience of such sculptures in their original architectural settings, though we have tried to suggest such in our gallery of Buddhist works. Those more fortunate may have the opportunity to visit the great cave-temple complexes in Honan, Shansi and Kansu provinces. There one can imaginatively recreate those periods when devotees and the religious community showed their faith by sponsoring monumental religious art of transcendent beauty.

Hsio-Yen Shih

99. Tomb Tile

Earthenware, solid grey body, surface
decorated with varied reliefs
impressed in clay by repetition of four
separate stamps—*feng-huang* bird on
border, archer on horseback shooting
at duck and overlapped hill motif on
upper register, two archers in front of
two-storied building in centre, and
monster-headed figure in military
costume holding sword below. Ht.
13¾" (34.7 cm.), w. 11½" (29 cm.),
thickness 1½" (3.6 cm.)
926.21.87

Later Han Dynasty, A.D. 2nd century.
Provenance:
Bishop W.C. White Collection.
Probably from Honan province.

100. Memorial Stele

Reddish grey sandstone, carved in low and high relief. Its main face's top panel has the scene of Prince Siddhārta's departure from Kapilavastu city in search of enlightenment which will lead to his becoming a Buddha, an Awakened One. Also unusual are a small panel showing a monkey perched on hills balancing two vestigial dragon-heads on the upper narrow ends proper right and left, two yakśas supporting flat stands for bodhisattvas flanking the central Buddha on the reverse face's top panel, and two discs below showing the sun-bird on the left and the moon-toad on the right. Inscriptions specifying the names of principal and secondary donors, mostly of the Chang clan, are incised beside panels with their pictorial symbolization. Beneath the dragonheads is a dedicatory inscription giving two cyclical days of the ninth month, the year being effaced but judged from such information to be A.D. 523, and the record that fifty-four people contributed to the stele's manufacture for the souls of four specifically named persons. Ht. 88½" (224.8 cm.), w. 27" (68.55 cm.), thickness 11" (27.95 cm.)
949.100

Northern Wei Dynasty, A.D. 523.

Published:
G. Salles, *Arts de la Chine ancienne* (Paris: Musée de l'Orangerie, 1937), p. 23 no. 14;
O. Sirén, "La sculpture chinoise a l'exposition de l'Orangerie," *Revue des Arts Asiatiques*, Tome XI (1937), Pl. I;
An Exhibition of Chinese Stone Sculpture (New York: C.T. Loo, 1940), no. 17;
H.E.Fernald, "A Chinese Buddhist Sculpture," ROMA *Bulletin*, No. 18 (March 1952), pp. 4-8;
T.A. Heinrich, *Art Treasures in the* ROM (Toronto, 1963), p. 39;
H. Trubner, *The Far Eastern Collection* (Toronto: ROM, 1968), p. 42 no. 45.
Cf. S. Mizuno & T. Nagahiro, *Yün-kang* (Kyoto: Jimbun kagaku kenkyūshō, 1955), Vol. III Pl. 35 & Vol. XV Pl. 101, for "Great Departure" scenes in reliefs on the east side of the south wall in Cave 6 and the lower east part of the north wall in Cave 41 at the great temple complex of northern Shansi province;
O. Sirén, *Chinese Sculptures in the von der Heydt Collection* (Zürich: Museum Rietberg, 1959), pp. 60-63, for a comparable stele dated to A.D. 520 from southern Shansi province.

101. Coffin Platform Side

Limestone, face carved in low modelled relief. Horizontal register with a frontal monster flanked by profile dragons and birds with everted heads, all coiled around and biting a double band. Central support with two warriors flanking a flower. Side supports with protective monsters.
Ht. 19⅜" (49.2 cm.), l. 82¾" (210.2 cm.)
949.230

Six Dynasties period, second half of 6th century A.D.

Published:
G. Salles, *Arts de la Chine ancienne* (Paris: Musée de l'Orangerie, 1937), p. 28 no. 28;
O. Sirén, "La sculpture chinoise a l'exposition de l'Orangerie," *Revue des Arts Asiatiques*, Tome XI (1937), Pl. III;
Chinese Sculpture (Portland: Art Museum, 1940), no. 5;
An Exhibition of Chinese Stone Sculpture (New York: C.T. Loo, 1940), no. 35;
T.A. Heinrich, *Art Treasures in the ROM* (Toronto, 1963), p. 38;
H. Trubner, *The Far Eastern Collection* (Toronto: ROM, 1968), p. 45 no. 49.
Cf. O. Sirén, *Chinese Sculpture in the van der Heydt Collection* (Zürich: Museum Rietberg, 1959), no. 5, for an earlier example of such a structure;
Teng Hsien ts'ai-se hua-hsiang-chuan mu (Peking: Wen-wu, 1958), colour plate, for a painted arched entrance to a tomb excavated at Teng Hsien, Honan province, which is both iconographically and stylistically similar.

102. Pillar Support

Limestone, carved in high relief. A kneeling demon figure with feline head and anthropoid body, winged and clawed animal paws instead of arms, and upper legs ending in spirals. Removed from rock-cut cave temples in the northern Hsiang-t'ang Shan complex, near the borders of Honan and Hopei provinces.
Ht. 31" (78.7 cm.)
960.92

Northern Ch'i Dynasty, 550-575.

Published:
H. Trubner, "A Demon from Hsiang-t'ang Shan," ROM *Annual*, 1961, pp. 73-74;
T.A. Heinrich, *Art Treasures in the ROM* (Toronto, 1963), p. 37;
H. Trubner, *The Far Eastern Collection* (Toronto, ROM, 1968), p. 43 no. 46.
Cf. S. Mizuno & T. Nagahiro, *The Buddhist Cave-temples of Hsiang-t'ang-ssu* (Kyoto: Tōhō-bunka, 1937), Pls. LVII & LVIII C-D, for such supports photographed *in situ*.

103. Head of Monk or Disciple of Buddha

Creamy white micaceous marble, carved in the round.
Ht. 6" (15.2 cm.).
960.239.6

Northern Ch'i Dynasty (550-577).
Provenance:
Dr. James M. Menzies Collection.

105. **Buddha** possibly **Amitābha**

Creamy white micaceous marble, carved in the round. Only its head is fully rounded, though without definition of hair at the back. The figure may originally have been attached to a wall or other background plane. Its back is flat and shows a single detail, the robe's end behind the left shoulder. Two squared tenon holes were cut between the shoulders and behind the knees. More enigmatic are two smaller conical holes in the broken side edges of the robe's hem, perhaps to hold restorations now lost. The figure stands on a small circular flat base, connected at the back with a vertical slab topped by an ogival arch. The base's conical bottom fits imperfectly with an inverted lotus socle. A dedicatory inscription with donors' names appears on three sides of the rectangular plinth and on the low drum above it. Its first three characters are indistinct but do not agree with those for the reign name and date equivalent to A.D. 577, as has usually been thought. They could be read as K'ai-huang 7 or A.D. 587. Three figures were dedicated at the time—of Amitābha, Avalokiteśvara and Mahāśthāmaprāpta.
Ht. 105¾"(268.6 cm.)
923.18.13

Sui Dynasty (581-618).
Provenance:
George Crofts Collection.
Reportedly from "Pu Lu Temple, Li Tsuan *(sic),"* P'ing-ting Chou, Shansi province, not far from the Hopei border.

Published:
O. Sirén, "Indian and other Influences in Chinese Sculpture," *Studies in Chinese Art and some Indian Influences* (London: India Society, 1936), p. 30, Pl. IX fig. 36;
O. Sirén, "Chinese Marble Sculptures of the Transition Period," *Bulletin of the Museum of Far Eastern Antiquities,* Stockholm, No. 12 (1940), pp. 479-481, Pl. II a;
L. Sickman and A. Soper, *The Art and Architecture of China* (Baltimore: Penguin, 1956), p. 59, Pl. 45A;
T.A. Heinrich, *Art Treasures in the ROM* (Toronto, 1963), p. 41;
H. Trubner, *The Far Eastern Collection* (Toronto: ROM, 1968), p. 44 no. 47;
W.K. Ho, "Notes on Chinese Sculpture from Northern Ch'i to Sui " *Archives of Asian Art,* Vol. XXII (1968-69), p. 10 fig. 6.
Cf. O. Sirén, "Chinese Marble Sculptures...," pp. 482, 494-495, Pls. III c and VIII c, for an Avalokiteśvara now in the Tokyo National Museum and an Amitābha in the British Museum, both of comparable style and related to A.D. 585 by inscription;
S. Matsubara, *Chinese Buddhist Sculpture* (Tokyo: Yoshikawa kōbunkan, 1961), Pl. 134, p. 242, for the same Tokyo sculpture and a transcription of an inscription on its plinth, stating that a Buddha and two bodhisattvas had been carved in A.D. 585 for the Ch'ung-kuang Temple which was ordered to be restored in 685.

106. **Lion**
Creamy white marble, carved in the
round.
Ht. 6-9/16" (16.8 cm.)
933.12.4

Sui-T'ang Dynasty, later 6th-early 7th
century.
Provenance:
Bishop W.C. White Collection.
Reportedly from Lo-yang,
Honan province.

107. Altarpiece

Gilt-bronze, cast in *cire perdue* technique. The whole is a composite of three distinct parts of different origin. The Buddha himself, probably Amitābha, and a 12-petalled lotus socle form one, terminating in a tenon below. The openwork mandorla with a frontal apsarases at its centre top, flanked by two small seated Buddhas, two more flying apsarases to either side, and originally supported by two caryatid figures, is fastened by a pin through the pierced projection between the Buddha's shoulders. The three tiered base bears an inscription on its sides and back, dated to A.D. 582. Base ht. 3⅜" (8.5 cm.), Buddha ht. 6" (15.2 cm.), mandorla ht. 6⅝" (16.8 cm.), assemblage ht. 12-3/7" (31.4 cm.)
958.81

Sui-T'ang Dynasty, late 6th-early 8th century.

Published:
H. Munsterberg, *Chinese Buddhist Bronzes* (Rutland, Vt: Charles E. Tuttle, 1967), p. 34, Pl. 26;
H. Trubner, *The Far Eastern Collection* (Toronto: ROM, 1968), p. 46 no. 51.
Cf. S. Matsubara, *Chinese Buddhist Sculpture* (Tokyo: Yoshikawa kōbunkan, 1961), Pl. 168b, p. 249, for a stone stele dated to A.D. 724, from the Pao-ch'ing Temple at Sian, Shensi province, comparable in style to the Buddha;
O. Sirén, *Chinese Sculpture* (London: Ernest Benn, 1925), Pl. 508, for a limestone stele dated to A.D. 664, reportedly from Shansi province, with apsaras of similar form.

108. Eleven-headed Kuan-Yin

(Ekādaśamukha Avalokiteśvara)
Gilt-bronze, cast in *cire perdue* technique. The bodhisattva has ten additional smaller heads arranged as a crown; five, three and one in ascending order, with a large one protruding from the back crown. Total ht. 9¼" (23.6 cm.)
970.349

T'ang Dynasty, 7th century.

Published:
S. Mizuno, "The Gilt Bronze Statuettes of Avalokiteśvara with Manifold Faces," *Ars Buddhica*, Vol. 10 (Dec. 1950), p. 89, Pl. 3B;
Chūgoku kodai chokoku ten (Tokyo: Takashimaya, 1959), C31;
S. Lee and W.K. Ho, "A Colossal Eleven-faced Kuan-yin of the T'ang Dynasty," *Artibus Asiae*, Vol. XXII (1959), fig. 4;
S. Matsubara, *Chinese Buddhist Sculpture* (Tokyo: Yoshikawa kōbunkan, 1961), Pl. 165a.

109. Bodhisattva

Buff-grey sandstone, carved in high relief. Originally cut from the living rock of a cave wall, the figure was removed and broken just below its knees. It had been the outer standing bodhisattva flanking the central Buddha's proper left in a group of five figures on the north wall of Cave 18 at the T'ien-lung Shan temple complex in Shansi province.
Ht. 29½" (69.85 cm.)
953.127

T'ang Dynasty, first half of 8th century.
Acquired through the Reuben Wells Leonard Bequest.

Published:
Ancient Chinese Bronzes and Buddhist Art (New York: Yamanaka, 1938), p. 58;
"West-East," ROMA *Bulletin*, No. 21 (Oct. 1953), p. 26 no. 109, Pl. 8;
H.E. Fernald, "A Buddhist Stone Sculpture from T'ien Lung Shan," ROMA *Bulletin*, No. 22 (Sept. 1954), pp. 1-3, fig. 1;
T.A. Heinrich, *Art Treasures in the* ROM (Toronto, 1963), p. 41;
H. Trubner, *The Far Eastern Collection* (Toronto: ROM , 1968), p. 45 no. 48.
Cf. H. Vanderstappen and M. Rhie, "The Sculpture of T'ien Lung Shan," *Artibus Asiae*, Vol. XXVII (1965), pp. 204-206, figs. 63-66, for discussion of the north wall, Cave 18, at T'ien-lung Shan. Heads of the central Buddha and standing bodhisattva proper right are now in the Nedzu Museum, Tokyo. The head of the seated bodhisattva proper left is in the Rijksmuseum voor Volkenkunde, Leiden; that for the seated bodhisattva proper right was formerly in the collection of Yamanaka & Co.

110. Monk

White marble, carved in the round; traces of red and blue pigments from original painted surface.
Ht. 66¾" (169.5 cm.)
922.20.95

Northern Sung Dynasty (960-1126).
Provenance:
George Crofts Collection.
Reportedly from a temple at Yang-ku (*sic*, probably Yang-kao near Ta-t'ung) Hsien, Shansi province.

Published:
T.A. Heinrich, *Art Treasures in the* ROM (Toronto, 1963), p. 54;
Man and His World, International Fine Arts Exhibition Catalogue, Expo 67, Montreal, p. 20 no. 10.
Cf. *Shensi-sheng po-wu-kuan shih-k'e hsüan-chi* (Peking: Wen-wu, 1957), p. 52 no. 49, for a headless figure of similar iconographic type;
Shansi shih-tiao i-shu (Peking: Ch'ao-hua mei-shu, 1962), no. 55, for another related headless figure showing the prevalence of this type in the Shansi-Shensi area;
R. Torii, *Culture of Liao Dynasty from Viewpoint of Archaeology* (Tokyo: Tōhō-bunka gakuin, 1936), Vol. I Pl. 41, Vol. II Pls. 152-153, Vol. III Pls. 246-249, for relief sculptures with comparable drapery stylizations from the Liao Dynasty imperial mausoleum complex of the first half of the 11th century, near Baling, eastern Mongolia.

111. Lohan (Arhat)

Earthenware; reddish-buff clay layer over coarser greyish clay core; body supported by grid-like rods of iron armature, arms by bundles of rush left as ash after firing; glazed in amber, green and yellow. His head is similar in material and technique to the body but appears different, its glaze being discoloured probably through water staining. He wears standard Chinese monastic garments except for one unusual feature, a head-cloth with end ties, tucked into the back collar and hanging to about the centre of his back. Ht. 49¾" (126.4 cm.) 914.4.1

Liao Dynasty, 12th century.
Gift of Mrs. H.D. Warren.
Reportedly found with a group of lohan in caves at I-chou, south of Peking, Hopei province. Others of the same find may be seen in the Museum of Fine Arts, Boston: Nelson Gallery-Atkins Museum, Kansas City; Metropolitan Museum, New York; University of Pennsylvania Museum, Philadelphia; and the British Museum, London.

Published:
T.A. Heinrich, *Art Treasures in the* ROM (Toronto, 1963), p. 55;
M. Wolf, "The Lohans from I-chou," *Oriental Art*, Vol. XV no. 1 (Spring 1969), p. 52, fig. 6;
H. Trubner, *The Far Eastern Collection* (Toronto: ROM, 1968), p. 63 no. 76.

114. **To-Wen** (Kubera or Vaiśravaṇa, Guardian of the North)
Limestone, carved in high relief. His left arm originally supported a stūpa, now effaced. A second attribute, banner or lance, should be held in his right hand which is here simply clenched. Two nude figures beneath his feet symbolize demons. Ht. 29¾" (75.5 cm.), w. 27" (68.6 cm.)
921.21.253

Yüan Dynasty, 14th century.
Provenance:
George Crofts Collection.
Reportedly from "She Kou Sze" (*sic*), a mountain temple in Honan province.

Published:
W.C. White, *Chinese Temple Frescoes* (Toronto: Univ. Press, 1940), fig. 28.
Cf. O. Sirén, *Chinese Sculpture* (London: Ernest Benn, 1925), Pl. 565, for two limestone reliefs of comparable size and format, the second of which is now in the Freer Gallery of Art, Washington, D.C., showing processions of bodhisattvas and musicians, supposedly from Shantung province but sometimes thought to be of the same sculptural complex as the To-wen;
Huan Yung-ch'üan, *Hang-chou Yüan-tai shih-k'u i-shu* (Peking: Chung-kuo ku-tien i-shu, 1958), Pl. 58, for a Mahākāla dated by inscription to A.D. 1322 and with similar facial stylizations, from the Pao-ch'eng Temple of Wu Shan near Hang-chou, Chechiang province.

115. Head of Pi-Hsia Yüan-Chün
(daughter of the Spirit of Mount T'ai)
Limestone, carved in the round. Her
crown is surmounted by a dove.
Ht. 15¼" (38.5 cm.)
921.31.24

Ming Dynasty, 15th century.
Provenance:
George Crofts Collection.
Gift of Mr. D.A. Dunlap.
Cf. O. Sirén, *Chinese Sculpture*
(London: Ernest Benn, 1925), Pl.
563B, for a very similar head,
reportedly from Shantung province;
Pei-ching Fa-hai Ssu Ming-tai pi-hua
(Peking: Chung-kuo ku-tien i-shu,
1958), Pls. 26, 31-33, for
comparable stylizations of eyes and
mouths in wall-paintings at the temple
of Fa-hai, built and decorated from
1439 to 1444 in the western suburbs
of Peking.

116. Yen-Lo Wang (Yama, President
of the Fifth Court of Hades)
Stoneware, buff body glazed in
amber, green and yellow. A signature
incised in the clay before firing, to the
rear of the base, reads "Made by Mr.
Ma." An ink inscription added after
firing bears the reign and year date
equivalent to A.D. 1524. Ht. 33" (83.8
cm.), w. 28" (71.1 cm.)
923.6.3

Ming Dynasty, 16th century.
Provenance:
George Crofts Collection.
Reportedly from Lu-an Fu,

Shansi province.

Published:
The Arts of the Ming Dynasty (Detroit:
Institute of Arts, 1952), no. 212;
T.A. Heinrich, *Art Treasures in the* ROM
(Toronto, 1963), pp. 62-63;
H. Trubner, *The Far Eastern Collection*
(Toronto: ROM, 1968), p. 57 no. 68.

117. Tomb Tiles

Earthenware cast in two-part moulds with hollow interior; grey body of well-fired fine clay; main surfaces decorated with pictorial compositions made up of several repeated stamped motifs. Scene of a hunt; a horse and rider pursuing a tiger, four repetitions of a phoenix. Ht. 18" (45.7 cm.), l. 44" (106.7 cm.)
931.13.128

Scene of attendant-figures in a landscape; five figures of which one is a repetition, three repetitions of a tree, two goose in flight designs of which one is repeated four and the other five times, five repetitions of a standing crane, and a single hound-dog. Ht. 21" (53.3 cm.), l. 63" (160.1 cm.).
931.13.137

Former Han Dynasty, 1st century B.C.
Provenance:
Bishop W.C. White Collection.
Reportedly from Mang-shan,
north of Lo-yang, Honan province.

Published:
W.C. White, *Tomb Tile Pictures of Ancient China* (Toronto: Univ. Press, 1939), Pls. 17 & 34.

118. Homage to the First Principle

Wall paintings; ink and water-soluble pigments applied over brush under-drawing; the wall base of rough mud mortar, covered with layer of finer clay and top coat of lime for painting ground. The two processional compositions originally, probably, stood on the east and west walls of a Taoist temple structure, with the main wall on the north. Ht. 10'5" (3 m. 6.5 cm.) and 10'4" (3 m. 4 cm.); w. 34'1" (10 m. 42.1 cm.) and 33'6½" (10 m. 25.4 cm.)
933.6.2-.3

Yüan Dynasty, later 13th-early 14th century.
Gift of the Flavelle Foundation in memory of Sir Joseph Flavelle.
Reportedly from southern Shansi province.

Published:
W.C. White, *Chinese Temple Frescoes* (Toronto: Univ. Press, 1940), pp. 164-226;
H.E. Fernald, "Chinese Frescoes from the ROM," ROMA *Bulletin*, Nos. 13-14 (Dec. 1945, Jan. 1946);
A. Giuganino, *La Pittura Cinese* (Rome: Istituto poligrafico dello stato, 1959), Pls. 274-5;
T.A. Heinrich, *Art Treasures in the ROM* (Toronto, 1963), pp. 60-61;
The Bishop White Gallery (Toronto: ROM, 1969), pp. 4-8.
Cf. *Yung-lo Kung pi-hua hsüan-chi* (Peking: Wen-wu, 1958), for wall paintings in a closely related style from a large temple complex near Jui-ch'eng, Shansi province;
Ch'in Ling-yün, *Chung-kuo pi-hua i-shu* (Peking: Chung-kuo ku-tien i-shu 1960), pp. 65-67, where these wall paintings are identified as from Lin-fen Hsien in southern Shansi;
Wen Wu, 1963 no. 8, p. 19 ff., for discussion of the iconographical complex of the Yung-lo Kung, which was rebuilt after a fire in A.D. 1262 and must have been completed before an inscription of A.D. 1325 on one of its walls.

120. Scholar in Summer Landscape by T'ang Yin (1470-1523)
Hanging scroll, painted in ink and slight colour on silk-satin. A 7-character 4-line poem and dedication are inscribed at the upper right—
"Rushing mountain streams and far-reaching road.
I cross the wilderness bridge in lonely wandering;
A forest of green trees in slanting rays,
Guess who traces these fluttering shadows.
T'ang Yin of Wu-yang painted this for Ch'eng-ch'i, Mr. Sung."
Three seals of the painter follow—cf. V. Contag and C.C. Wang, *Maler-und Sammler-Stempel aus der Ming-und Ch'ing-Zeit* (Shanghai: Commercial, 1940), p. 227, nos. 10, 11 and 15. Ht. 53½" (135.9 cm.), w. 21⅜" (54.3 cm.)
957.19

Ming Dynasty, first quarter of 16th century.
Provenance:
Hsïang Yüan-pien (1525-1590)—cf. Contag and Wang, *op. cit.*, pp. 610-612, nos. 9, 10, 25, 32, 59, 61 and 66, 8 seals total;
Weng Sung-nien (1647-1728)—"Sung-nien tsu-shang" and "Wu-lin Weng-shih shu-hua chi", 2 seals;
Wang Lan-sheng (1679-1737)—"T'an-chai shu-hua", 1 seal;
Li Tsung-wan (1705-1759)—*Ibid.*, p. 622, nos. 9, 12, 15, 21 and 23, 5 seals;
Ch'in T'ung-li (20th century)—"T'ung-li chen-tsang", 1 seal;
Wang Chi-ch'ien (20th century)—"Ts'eng-tsang Wang Chi-ch'ien ch'u," 1 seal;
also 3 unidentified seals—"Tung-lin ch'ing-yin", "Fu-p'ing ssu-yin" and "Ch'ung-yin-an chu"; and 2 indecipherable ones.

Published:
H.C. Tseng, *Loan Exhibition of Chinese Paintings* (Toronto: ROM, 1956), No. 18;
H. Trubner, "A Painting by T'ang Yin," ROM *Annual*, 1959, pp. 46-49;
1000 Jahre chinesische Malerei (Munich: Haus der Kunst, 1960), p. 82 no. 46;
S.E. Lee, *Chinese Landscape Painting*, 2nd ed. rev. (Cleveland: Museum of Art, 1962), p. 64 no. 49;
T.A. Heinrich, *Art Treasures in the ROM* (Toronto, 1963), p. 64;
H. Trubner, *The Far Eastern Collection* (Toronto: ROM, 1968), p. 21 no. 10.

山氣決決路迢迢惆悵間
行過野橋緣樹一林斜
日裏飄些巾影倩誰
橋吳揚唐寅為
成嵩宋君畫

121. **Portrait**
Hanging scroll, painted in ink and colours on coarse silk. An inscription at its upper right identifies the subject—"An image of Mr. Yang, posthumous name Mao-lin, District Examination Graduate of the Ming." Ht. 64" (162.6 cm.), w. 14¼" (106 cm.)
921.1.150

Ming Dynasty, 16th century.
Provenance:
George Crofts Collection.
Compare the carved *ju-i* scroll ornament on its horseshoe-armchair ends and footstool with a *guri* lacquer tray of the mid-16th century (see No. 137); and the stylized cloud pattern on the young man's blue damask robe with such designs on porcelains decorated in underglaze blue, of the Chia-ching through Wan-li periods (1522-1619).

122. **Lotus** by Chou Ch'üan (18th century)
Hanging scroll, painted in ink on paper. An inscription at the upper left gives a poem and the painter's signature—
"Dried lotus stalks hem the autumn pond,
A border of beauties preening within its mirror;
Clouds flying in their red abode, the birds rejoice together;
No need to seek elsewhere for the Hsiao and Hsiang.
Described in the ninth month of autumn, 1727, by Chü-heng, Chou Ch'üan."
Two seals of the painter follow—"Chou Ch'üan ssu-yin" and "Chü-heng." Two seals of an unidentified collector appear at the lower right—"Huang-kang I-chuang Wang-shih chen-tsang" and "Fa-i chih tsang." Ht. 97⅜" (245.8 cm.), w. 34⅛" (86.4 cm.).
971.128

Ch'ing Dynasty, Yung-cheng period, 1727.

123. **Portrait**

Hanging scroll, painted in ink and colours on paper. Two eulogies of its subject, in Chinese on the right and Manchu on the left, are inscribed on a separate piece of paper and mounted above the painting proper. These are dated to A.D. 1760 and were presented to the Emperor Kao-tsung by three officials, Liu T'ung-hsün (1700-1773), Liu Lun (1711-1773) and Yü Min-chung (1714-1780). Tan-pa-pa-t'u-lu-na-mu-ch'a-erh, Imperial Bodyguard of the Second Class, was honoured for his victory in a skirmish with Muslim rebels. Ht. with inscription 73-7/16" (186.5 cm.), w. 37⅜" (95 cm.)
923x56.8

Ch'ing Dynasty, Ch'ien-lung period, 1760.

124. **The Scribe** by Kai Ch'i (1774-1829)

Hanging scroll, painted in ink and slight colour on silk. An inscription on the upper right gives the painter's signature—*"The seventh month of autumn, 1827, in imitation of Yüan artists' brushwork, by Ch'i-hsiang, Kai Ch'i."* Two seals of the painter follow. Ht. 30⅛" (76.3 cm.), w. 16⅜" (41.4 cm.)
921.21.22

Ch'ing Dynasty, Tao-kuang period, 1827.
Provenance:
George Crofts Collection.

二等侍衛丹巴
巴圖魯那木查
爾

于思棄甲誰當一
隊徑率百人攻其
腹背手取囬礮回
膽盡寒鋹繡糢糊
橫捎左鞍

乾隆庚辰春月既望御題并書

勒恭讚

125. **"Bamboo House at the Yellow Gorge"** by Ch'ien Tu (1763-1844) Two album leaves mounted on a single hanging scroll, painted in ink and slight colour on paper. The painting has its artist's seal at the lower right—cf. V. Contag and C.C. Wang, *Maler-und Sammler-Stempel aus der Ming-und Ch'ing-Zeit* (Shanghai: Commercial, 1940), p. 464, no. 13. The inscription copies a record by Chü Chieh, a follower of Wen Cheng-ming (1470-1559), who eulogized his place of enforced retirement as a demoted official in 1599. Chü also painted a long handscroll of his retreat in the countryside of Hupei province. Remembering and admiring this earlier work, Ch'ien imitated it in his own country place, just before New Year in 1828. Another seal is impressed towards the close of his inscription—cf. *Ibid*, p. 464, no. 21. Ht. of painting 9¼" (23.5 cm.), w. of painting 10½" (26.6 cm.)
969.15.1

Ch'ing Dynasty, Tao-kuang period, 1828.
Provenance:
Tomioka Tessai Collection.

Published:
O. Sirén, *A History of Later Chinese Painting* (London: Medici Society, 1938), Vol. II, p. 242;
T. Naito, *Shina kaigashi* (Tokyo: Kōbundo, 1938), opposite p. 176;
S.E. Lee, *Chinese Landscape Painting,*

2nd ed. rev. (Cleveland: Museum of Art, 1962), p. 133 no. 108.

Jade

The ROM's collection of Chinese jade numbers about one thousand pieces, of the widest possible range and variety. As Currelly put it (*I Brought the Ages Home*; Toronto: Ryerson, 1956), "(George) Crofts got very little that was B.C. and (Bishop William C.) White very little that was A.D., so that now both periods are well represented in the Museum." A third important group of jades was given by Dr. James M. Menzies. In it are fine, whole, generally archaic specimens, and numerous fragments of value for their reported provenance or for technical study and mineralogical testing by X-ray diffraction and other kinds of analysis.

Toronto is strongest in the jades of the Eastern Chou Dynasty. The number of disks, pendants, and beads with the spiral pattern alone, for example, allows close stylistic analysis of a pattern which was almost diagnostic for the period (see No. 127). Also numerous are the larger and more spectacular jades of the last of Ch'ing Dynasty—vessels, imperial seals, sculpture, etc. The number of pieces in the ROM from that time between the Han and Ch'ing Dynasties, called the "dark millennium" for jade studies due to the paucity of archaeological evidence from datable tombs, has only recently been noted (Nos.130 and131).

Of the various types of jade, ritual jades (*pi* disks, *tsung* prisms, *kuei* and *chang* sceptres, etc.) are well represented. Mostly of this type and including both archaic and archaistic examples, are the ten or so jades purchased by Bishop White from the collection of the great early jade scholar, Wu Ta-ch'eng (1835-1902). In the weapons and tools category are numerous axes and *ko* halberds (see No. 126) ranging in size from amuletic miniatures of less than one inch to a blade (originally) about 16 inches long. Personal ornaments are best represented by the Chin-ts'un jades acquired by Bishop White near the find spot, "Old Loyang" in Honan. There is a (Crofts) group of nearly one hundred rectangular plaques of jade and jade-like stones, whose use can only now be realistically estimated, due to the recent discovery of the jade-encased Prince and his Consort of the Western Han Dynasty in an undisturbed cliff tomb at Man-ch'eng in Hopei Province. Sculpture includes smaller and large examples from the first to last dynasties; the most important or best known example in the ROM, the black water-buffalo (No. 129), being updated here from the traditional Shang to a Han Dynasty date. The lotus cup (No. 134) is one of the finer and early examples of that branch of sculpture represented by the carving of jade vessels, which was done in ceramic and archaistic as well as naturalistic forms.

"Chinese jade" in the strict sense does not, so far as is known, exist, for neither nephrite nor jadeite has yet been quarried within the confines of China proper. The term is the result, rather, of millennia of arduous importation, love and work resulting in a supreme mystery of form and technique.

Doris Dohrenwend

193

126. **Dagger-axe** *(ko)* **Blade**
Jade; ivory coloured, with gold and
brown staining; traces of calcification;
rejoined blade translucent only at
thinnest edges; cylindrical
perforation. Traces of earth and red
pigment. L. 12⅞" (32.6 cm.)
934.17.119

Shang Dynasty, Anyang period (*c.*
1300-1028 B.C.).
Provenance:
Bishop W.C. White Collection.
Reportedly discovered near Ta-
ssu-k'ung-ts'un, An-yang, Honan
province, with bronzes, etc. from the
"Elephant Tomb" group.

Published:
W.C. White, *Bronze Culture of Ancient
China* (Toronto: Univ. Press, 1956), p.
53, Pl. XVII :A;
D. Dohrenwend, *Chinese Jades in the
ROM* (Toronto, 1971), p. 46 right.

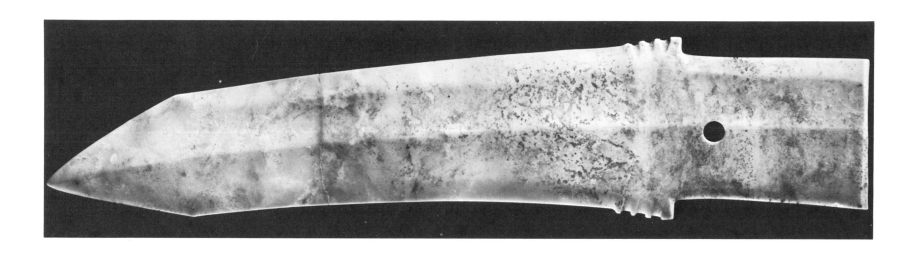

127. **Dragon Pendant**
Jade; faintly translucent yellow-green
and brown, one face almost
completely brown with traces of
calcification. Body carved on both
sides with spiral, "C" and "S" forms in
strong relief; jaws lined with finely
striated bands. L. 5" (12.7 cm.)
931.13.16

Eastern Chou Dynasty, *c.* 5th century B.C.
Provenance:
Bishop W.C. White Collection.
Reportedly from Chin-ts'un,
Honan province.

Published:
W.C. White, *Tombs of Old Loyang*
(Shanghai: Kelly & Walsh, 1934), Pl.
LXXVI, no. 313B;
H. Trubner, *The Far Eastern Collection*
(Toronto: ROM, 1968), p. 31 no. 28;
D. Dohrenwend, *Chinese Jades in the
ROM* (Toronto, 1971), p. 7.
Cf. A. Salmony, *Carved Jades of
Ancient China* (Berkeley: Gillick,
1938), Pl. XLII : 4.

130. Headpiece, Girdle Pendant Set

Jade; translucent white plaque; three neat cylindrical perforations, slightly concave border band. Mythical stag and plant in very low relief; stylized clouds incised. Traces of earth.
L. 3-7/16" (8.7 cm.)
927.19.150

Six Dynasties period, 6th century.
Provenance:
Bishop W.C. White Collection.

Published:
D. Dohrenwend, *Chinese Jades in the* ROM (Toronto, 1971), p. 100.
Cf. *K'ao-ku*, 1962 no. 4, p. 195 fig. 4:1, for jade pendant plaques from a 5th or 6th century tomb in Kiangsi province.

131. Comb Top

Jade; translucent white; thin with convex, concave and engraved designs on both faces. Lotus leaf on reverse supports a pair of finely cross-hatched fish. Traces of earth. L. 3⅛" (7.9 cm.)
927.19.149

Sung Dynasty (960-1279).
Provenance:
Bishop W.C. White Collection.

Published:
D. Dohrenwend, *Chinese Jades in the* ROM (Toronto, 1971), p. 106.
Cf. *K'ao-ku t'ung-hsün*, 1955 no. 6, p. 62 fig. 4, for a Sung bronze mirror with a similar design.

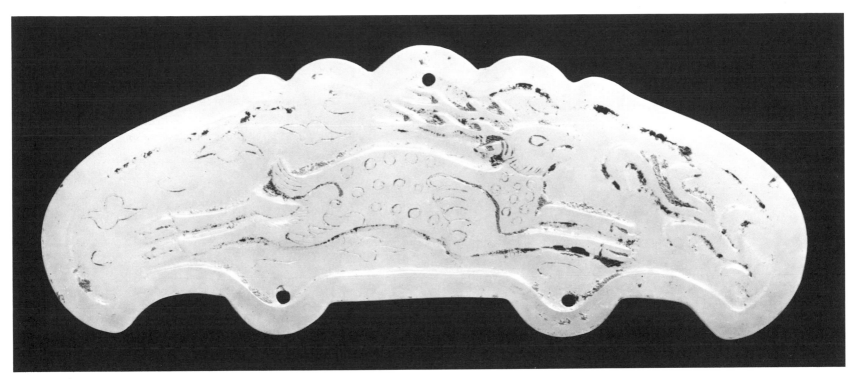

133. Fu Dog

Jade; semi-translucent grey with grey-to-black veins and occasional amber tinge or vein, low but fine polish. Large, square-jawed head shows brow and beard curls, teeth and tongue; facetted claws; tripartite tail in finely striated relief on animal's left flank; three breast folds. L. 6" (15.2 cm.)
918.21.683

Ming Dynasty (1368-1644).
Provenance:
George Crofts Collection.

Published:
D. Dohrenwend, *Chinese Jades in the ROM* (Toronto, 1971), p. 112.

134. Lotus Cup

Jade; oyster-white, tinged with gold and grey; amber shadow about wavy rim (refinished at one point); semi-translucent where thinnest. Ht. 2" (5.1 cm.), l. 5¼" (13.3 cm.)
927.19.211

Ming Dynasty (1368-1644).
Provenance:
Bishop W.C. White Collection.

Published:
D. Dohrenwend, *Chinese Jades in the ROM* (Toronto, 1971), p. 116.
Cf. *Wen Wu*, 1964 no. 12, p. 58 fig. 17, an earlier cup, also with plastic detail (leaf) on underside, from a Yüan Dynasty tomb in Kiangsu province.

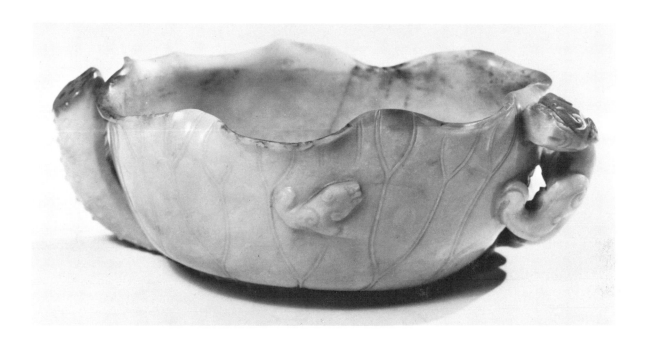

Lacquer

Probably of Chinese origin and known as early as Shang times at Anyang, the art of preserving and decorating wood and other surfaces with lacquer was perfected in the Warring States period. Intricately carved lacquer (see No. 136) or lacquered wood is known at least from Warring States times. Fragments of plain and painted lacquer from this early period on wood, pottery and hemp bases can be studied at the ROM. Shell-inlaid black lacquer, exquisite in the 17th century *laque burgautée* box (No. 138), is known from China as early as the 8th century B.C. The *"guri"* or *hsi-p'i* style of carving represented by the rectangular tray (No. 137) now appears based upon a Sung and Yüan Dynasty tradition of hammered metalwork.

The collection is richest, however, in carved red lacquers (see No. 135) of the 17th through 19th centuries, which display the greatest technical virtuosity and surface richness. These pieces range in size from writing brushes to very large rectangular and flattened spherical boxes. They include jade-inlaid discoidal palace table screens and a poetry cabinet from the Ch'ien-lung reign (1736-1795), as well as vases of current and archaistic types. Most of the treasures on view in the Lacquer Alcove are due to the generosity of Mrs. H.D. Warren and to the gift of the Dorothy and (Major) James E. Hahn Collection.

Doris Dohrenwend

136. Hexagonal Dish

Red and green lacquer sharply carved
to a reddish-gold ground over fibre-
covered wood base. Six character
Chia-ching (1522-1566) mark
carved in base. Believed to be one of a
set. Ht. 1½" (3.8 cm.), w. 7½" (19
cm.)
961.201.2

Ming Dynasty, Chia-ching mark and
period (1522-1566).

Published:
H. Trubner, "Ming Lacquer in the
Royal Ontario Museum," ROM *Annual*
1962, pp. 40-41, Pl. XVIII.
Cf. F. Low-Beer, "Chinese Lacquer of
the Middle and Late Ming Period,"
*Bulletin of the Museum of Far Eastern
Antiquities,* Stockholm, No. 24
(1952), Pls. I, II, X & XLII.

137. Tray

Dark *hsi-p'i (guri)* lacquer, carved deeply from brownish surface to dark ground; upper layers brown alternating with five of dark gold, lower layers darker brown or black alternating with four thin red layers. Recessed rectangular base with black lacquer reinforced by two transverse bars. "Crackle" of lacquer on base reveals coarse hemp-covered wood basis. Ht. 2" (5.2 cm.), l. 19½" (49.5 cm.), w. 13¾" (34.9 cm.)
966.218

Ming Dynasty, 16th century.
Cf. Sir Harry Garner, "Guri Lacquer of the Ming Dynasty," *Transactions of the Oriental Ceramic Society*, Vol. XXXI (1957-1959), Pl. 17b, "black" *guri*, Type B.

138. Three-Tiered Box

Black lacquer over hemp-covered, light wood frame; inlaid with mother-of-pearl; interior lacquered red. Lid top with scene of gentlemen and attendant in pavilion by shore with moored sampan. Ht. 10¾" (27.4 cm.), 9½" (24.2 cm.) square.
967.247.1 ABC.

Late Ming Dynasty, early 17th century.
Cf. J. Figgess, "Mother-of-Pearl Decorated Ming Lacquer: Some Clues to Dating," *Oriental Art*, XIV :3 (Autumn 1968), p. 164, a slightly earlier example of similar type.

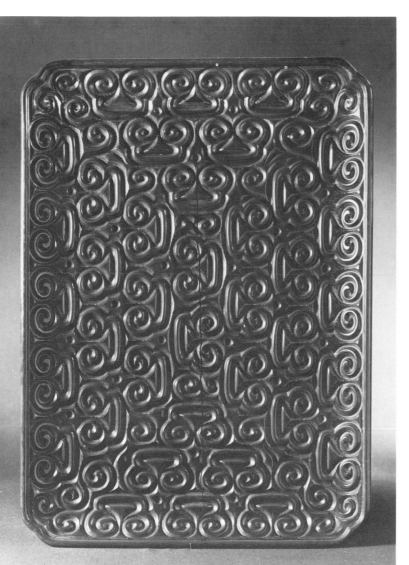

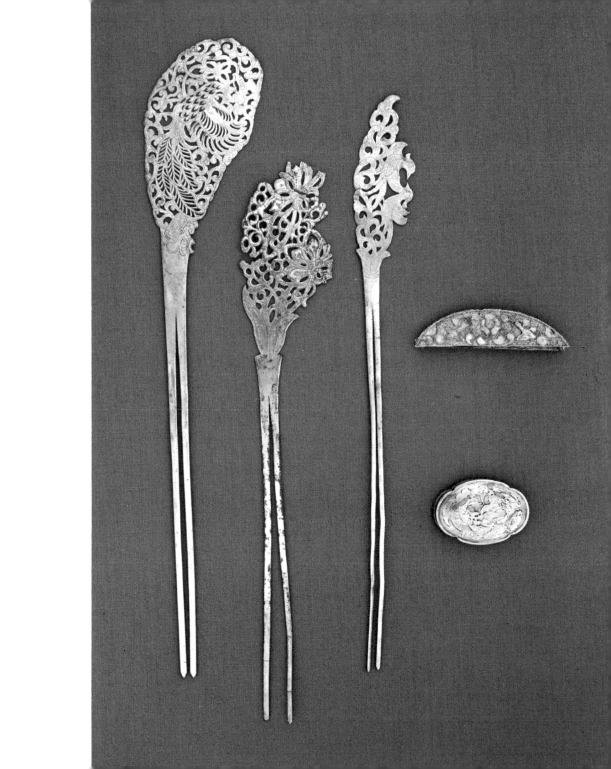

139. Stem Cup
Gilt bronze; traced design with ring-
matted ground. Ht. 2-9/16" (6.5 cm.)
950.36.3

T'ang Dynasty, 7th-8th century.

Published:
M. Sullivan, *Introduction to Chinese
Art* (London: Faber, 1961), p. 130;
H. Trubner, *The Far Eastern Collection*
(Toronto: ROM, 1968), p. 52 no. 61.
Cf. B. Gyllensvard, *Chinese Gold and
Silver in the Carl Kempe Collection*
(Stockholm: Nordisk, 1953), no. 109,
for a similar cup also in gilt bronze;
Wen Wu, 1972 no. 1, p. 39 fig. 19
shows a similar stem cup made of
silver, found in 1970 at Ho-chia-ts'un,
a southern suburb of Sian, Shensi
province.

140. **Comb Top**
Gold; design of mandarin ducks,
flowers and leaves outlined by
cloisons; background covered with
fine granulation. L. 2-31/32" (7.5
cm.)
959.120.1

T'ang Dynasty, 7th-8th century.
Cf. B. Gyllensvard, *Chinese Gold and
Silver in the Carl Kempe Collection*
(Stockholm: Nordisk, 1953), no. 37,
for side panels from a comb top with
cloisons still containing some
turquoise inlay, and almost identical
but inverted design;
Gift of Mrs. Edgar J. Stone.

Published:
H. Trubner, *The Far Eastern Collection*
(Toronto: ROM, 1968), p. 53 no. 63.
P. Singer, *Chinese Gold and Silver*
(New York: China Institute in America,
1971), no. 67, for side panels from a
similar piece in the Metropolitan
Museum of Art, New York.

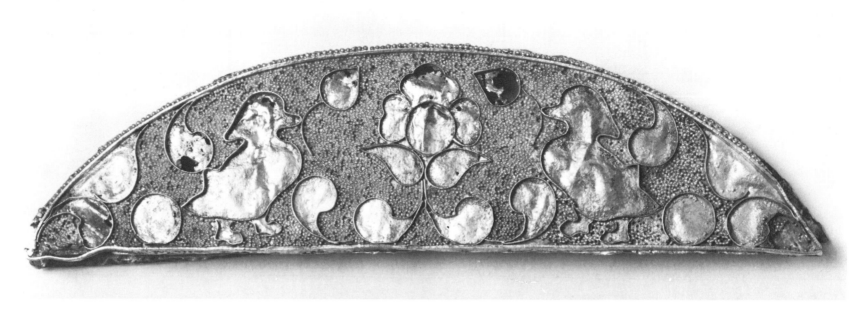

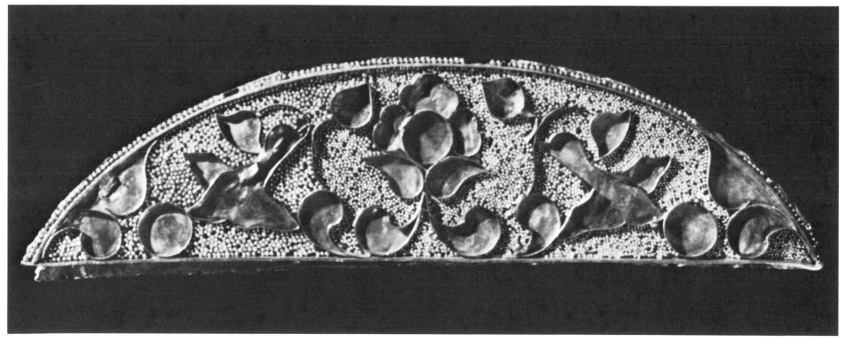

141. **Hairpin**
Silver with gilded head; repoussé
openwork design with traced details.
L. 12⅞" (32.7 cm.)
959.117.2

T'ang Dynasty, 8th-9th century.
Gift of Mrs. Edgar J. Stone.

Published:
T.A. Heinrich, *Art Treasures in the ROM*
(Toronto, 1963), pp. 48-49;
H. Trubner, *The Far Eastern Collection*
(Toronto: ROM , 1968), p. 53 no. 64.
Cf. B. Gyllensvard, "T'ang Gold and
Silver," *Bulletin of the Museum of Far
Eastern Antiquities*, Stockholm, No. 29
(1957), fig. 51c, a similar hairpin in
the Minneapolis Institute of Arts.

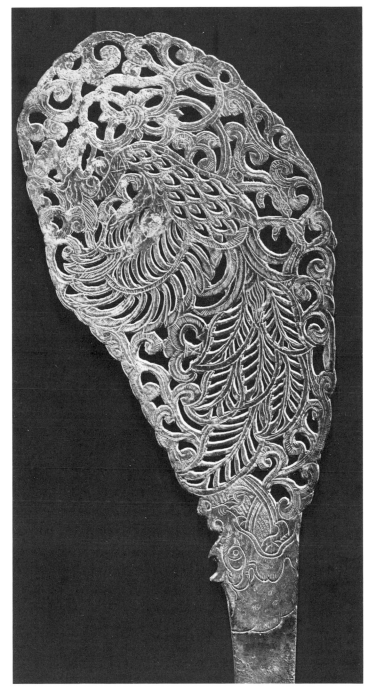

142. Hairpin
Silver with gilded head; repoussé
openwork design with traced details.
L. 11½" (29.3 cm.)
959.117.3

T'ang Dynasty, 8th-9th century.
Gift of Mrs. Edgar J. Stone.

Published:
T.A. Heinrich, *Art Treasures in the* ROM
(Toronto, 1963), pp. 48-49.
Cf. B. Gyllensvard, *Chinese Gold and
Silver in the Carl Kempe Collection*
(Stockholm: Nordisk, 1953), no. 126,
for a pair of hairpins with similar
decoration.

143. Hairpin
Silver with gilded head; repoussé
openwork design with traced details.
L. 11¼" (28.7 cm.)
918.7.175

T'ang Dynasty, 8th-9th century.
Provenance:
George Crofts Collection.
Cf. *K'ao Ku,* 1959 no. 12, p. 669, for
hairpins with openwork heads found
in a T'ang Dynasty tomb at Huang-ti-
kang, Canton, Kwangtung province,
together with coins of the K'ai-yüan
period (713-742), suggesting a date
before the middle of the 8th century;
Wen Wu, 1959 no. 8, p. 34 fig. 7, for
hairpins with openwork heads from
Hui-chia-ts'un in the southern
suburbs of Sian, Shensi province,
dated to the 2nd year of the T'ai-
chung period, A.D. 848.

144. Appliqué
Gold; repoussé design; probably
made for attachment to wooden box.
L. 5" (12.8 cm.)
925x64.6

T'ang Dynasty or later, 8th-10th
century.

145. **Covered Box**
Silver; traced and with parcel-gilt
design. L. 1¾" (4.45 cm.)
957.152.1

T'ang Dynasty or later, 8th-10th
century.
Cf. *Wen Wu*, 1955 no. 5, p. 34 nos. 4
& 6, p. 35 nos. 1 & 2, for a parcel-
gilt silver box of similar shape found at
Hung-ch'ing-ts'un, south-east of
Sian, Shensi province.

Textiles

The silks of China have been appreciated and prized in both the East and West since ancient times. During the Han Dynasty these precious stuffs reached imperial Rome along the famed silk road. However, textile impressions in patinas of bronze ritual vessels demonstrate that silk had been known and used since the Bronze Age, as several examples in the ROM collection affirm. Although comparatively recent in terms of China's textile history, the Museum's collection of Chinese costumes and furnishings reflects traditional technical skills and designs in weaving and embroidery. This collection is among the largest in North America and is internationally known for its holdings of Ch'ing dynasty court robes.

The oldest pieces in the collection are from the Ming Dynasty. Among these is a large *k'o-ssu* (silk tapestry) hanging depicting a Taoist paradise below a pair of confronted phoenix. It is a well-known, but rare, type made for the use of an empress and probably dates from the 16th century. No Ming costume is preserved in Western collections, but the ROM possesses an important, and apparently unique, panel made from four widths of velvet intended for an imperial robe (No. 146). It is among the earliest examples of Chinese velvet weaving, and although never made up into a garment, serves as a major document for study of the dragon robe which evolved from a semi-formal coat to become the Chinese official's costume.

The rise of Manchu power and the founding of the Ch'ing dynasty in the 17th century witnessed the introduction of costume styles based on a tight-sleeved, body-fitting riding coat, in contrast to flowing Ming style robes. Following the Ming, Manchu traditions included the Chinese custom of decorating clothing with dragons. The oldest surviving Ch'ing period dragon robe (see No. 147) marks a transition between older and newer modes. Its design retains traces of Ming-style drawing, but its impressive embroidery reflects the vitality of early Ch'ing period styles.

By the mid-18th century Manchu court costume was formally codified. Sizes, types, and positions of the nine dragons displayed on a cloud-filled field above a border depicting the earth mountain rising out of waves were prescribed by imperial edict, as well as the colours and accessories appropriate for each court rank.

By 1759 the Ch'ien-lung emperor made further concessions to Chinese traditions by adding to the imperial costume, the twelve ancient symbols of imperial authority worn by Chinese emperors since Han times. The colour yellow, the five-clawed dragon, and the five-coloured clouds had been reserved for the Manchu imperial family, but the twelve symbols placed at the shoulders, waist and knees of the dragon robe remained the prerogative of the emperor alone. Ten of these robes, including a twice-lengthened robe of the Ch'ien-lung emperor (No. 148), are preserved in the collection. Although an emperor could select any colour for his clothing, most of the surviving twelve symbols robes are yellow. A rare *k'o-ssu* robe worked entirely in shades of blue and white dating from the reign of the Tao-kuang emperor probably marks a specific court function (No. 149). It could have been appropriate wear during the period of fasting preceding sacrifices at the Altar of Heaven.

The decline of imperial authority and the economic collapse besetting 19th century China affected the quality and workmanship of late Ch'ing dragon robes, but informal robes associated with the private court of the Empress Dowager, Tz'u-hsi, are among the loveliest of Chinese costumes. Here the quality of traditional court embroidery was preserved a while longer in the refined ambience which prized colour harmonies and naturalistic designs matched to the nuances of seasonal variations. Over twenty garments in the collection purport to be from the wardrobe of the Empress Dowager, although in most cases this fact cannot be verified. The chrysanthemum and butterfly robe (No. 150) presents a design known to have been favoured by her, and is of such superb quality that only the empress would have dared wear it.

John Vollmer

146. **Panel**
Cut and uncut yellow silk velvet (solid
cicelé) embroidered in coloured silks
and gold filé. Piece consists of four
widths for imperial court robe *(ch'ao-
fu)*. L. 9'3-25/32" (309 cm.), w. 8'11-
11/16" (272 cm.)
956.67.2

Ming Dynasty, early 17th century.
Gift of Mrs. Edgar J. Stone.

Published:
K. Brett, "A Ming Dragon Robe," ROMA
Bulletin, No. 27 (June 1958), pp. 9-
14, Pl. 12, figs. 1-2;
H. Burnham, *Chinese Velvets,*   ROM
Occasional Papers No. 2 (1959), pp.
31-34, Pls. IV - V;
"Un velours impérial chinois d'epoque
Ming." *Bulletin de liaison du CIETA,* No.
9 (January 1959), pp. 53-60.

147. **Dragon Robe** *(chi-fu),* probably
for imperial consort
Yellow silk tabby ground completely
covered with embroidery in red and
yellow gold filé couching, and shaded
in blue, green, red and yellow satin
stitch. L. 54¾" (139 cm.)
919.6.21

Ch'ing Dynasty, K'ang-hsi Period, late
17th century.
Provenance:
George Crofts Collection.
Gift of the Robert Simpson Company.

Published:
H.E. Fernald, *Chinese Court
Costumes* (Toronto: ROM , 1946), no.
28, Pl. I ;
S. Camann, *China's Dragon Robes*
(New York: Ronald, 1952), Pl. 5.

148. **Imperial Twelve Symbol Dragon Robe** *(chi-fu)*
Pale yellow silk twill with satin and split stitch embroidery in shades of blue, brown, green, pink, red and yellow.
L. 57½" (146 cm.)
909.12.2

Ch'ing Dynasty, Ch'ien-lung Period, mid 18th century.

Published:
H.E. Fernald, *Chinese Court Costumes* (Toronto, ROM , 1946), no. 2, Pls. II & III, Col. Pl. B.

149. Imperial Twelve Symbol Dragon Robe *(chi-fu)*
Blue and white *k'o-ssu* (silk tapestry).
L. 57" (144.8 cm.)
919.6.3

Ch'ing Dynasty, Tao-kuang Period
(1821-1850).
Provenance:
George Crofts Collection.
Gift of the Robert Simpson Company.

Published:
H.E. Fernald, *Chinese Court Costumes* (Toronto: ROM , 1946), no. 7, Pl. IX

150. Woman's Informal Autumn Robe
Blue satin densely embroidered with couched gold filé, and satin stitch in shades of blue, green, orange, violet, yellow and white. L. 53½" (135.9 cm.)
919.6.128

Ch'ing Dynasty, *c.* 1900.
Provenance:
George Crofts Collection.
Gift of the Robert Simpson Company.
Reportedly from the wardrobe of the Dowager Empress, Tz'u-hsi.

Published:
H.E. Fernald, *Chinese Court Costumes* (Toronto: ROM, 1946), no. 70, Colour Pl. D.

Chinese Art was designed by Scott Thornley, Information Services, ROM, with photography by the Photography Department of the ROM. It is photoset by Moore Type Limited of Toronto in Univers Light, and was printed and bound by The Hunter Rose Company, Toronto, on 90 lb. Carlyle Japan stock with Kinwashi handmade endpapers. The publication was assisted by a grant from the Canada Council.